MASTER BUILDER ROBLOX

THE ESSENTIAL GUIDE

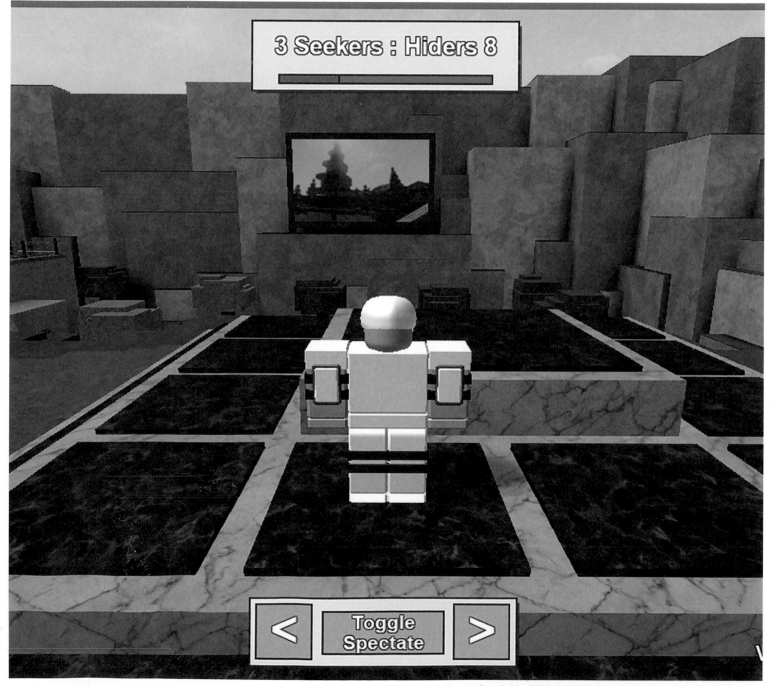

No part of this publication may be reproduced, stored in a retrieval system, or transmitted in any form
by any means, electronic, mechanical, photocopying, or otherwise, without prior written permission of the publisher,
Triumph Books LLC, 814 North Franklin Street; Chicago, Illinois 60610.

This book is book is available in quantity at special discounts for your group or organization.
For further information, contact:

Triumph Books LLC
814 North Franklin Street
Chicago, Illinois 60610
Phone: (312) 337-0747
www.triumphbooks.com

Printed in U.S.A.
ISBN: 978-1-62937-515-1

Content packaged by Mojo Media, Inc.
Joe Funk: Editor
Jason Hinman: Creative Director
Samantha Skinner: Senior Writer
Gerry Walsh: Contributing Writer

Jack Hinman: Engineering Consultant
Also special thanks to: Jane Funk, Mary Elizabeth Ebey, Chloe Leppink

CONTENTS

MASTER BUILDER ROBLOX

INTRODUCTION

RobloxFun12333 has joined the game.
Pojrm: follow
bubbaman1031 has joined the game.

bubbaman1031   bella7x

Play

Music by @KyleAllenMusic

AND WHERE TO FIND IT

Learning what you can do and where to get Roblox is a great place to start!

INTRODUCTION AND WHERE TO FIND IT

Imagine a world where whatever you think can come to life. Your ideas are literally living breathing things that you and your friends can experience. It doesn't matter if you want to be a pirate pillaging the seas, a vampire slayer fighting a horde of zombies, a guy chilling in his mansion or anything in between. Roblox is about making dreams come true and bringing ideas to life. Roblox is an interactive game that provides kids with a fun, safe way to build, explore new worlds and make friends.. With endless creative possibilities available to you, what will you build?

Create and customize your own character, build your own world or visit countless others, make friends or meet with friends you already know and chat with them in a whole new realm. With so many possibilities, there's always something to do in Roblox!

With the power to create a world of your own, what are you going to build? How will you run your world? Let your creativity free and watch it flow right onto your screen before you. Marvel at the creations you piece together. You can bring your creations to life and then play in them with your friends.

Whether you want to build a mansion to live in, a row of stores to make customers happy, a game that visitors have to learn to beat, your own mystery island or more; you can create just about anything when you use the builder to your advantage.

Made just for kids like you that want to control their own worlds, but also build their own ideas; you are the master in control. Create a character and begin playing today.

WHAT WILL YOU NEED TO PLAY ROBLOX

Roblox works on multiple operating systems, giving you the choice to play no matter what computer you're using. Windows Vista and higher is recommended for PC's and 10.7 or higher for Mac's. There is also a mobile Roblox platform that works on newer smartphones, so you can play Roblox on the go!

You'll need an internet connection to play Roblox smoothly. It's required because the game is played completely through web browsers and downloaded software on your computer itself.

Signing up is easy, free and you can meet up with all your friends that are playing online right now.

SIGNING UP FOR ROBLOX

Roblox is completely free to get and play. All you have to do is sign up with the website to get started.

Type in www.Roblox.com in the search bar of your web browser. *Make sure you get your parents' permission first!*

Sign up in the provided box — username, password, birthday, girl or boy. Accept the terms of use and get started!

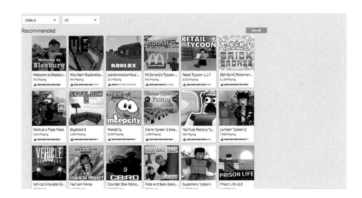

Signing up is easy to do and you can get right into the worlds once you have a user name. You'll see your HOME page each time you go to the Roblox website, letting you track your account.

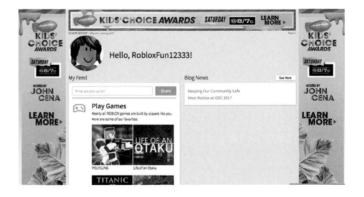

Navigating the home page is easy. Everything is laid out in front of you to choose from.

Notifications provide you with a way to see if any notices, alerts or messages were left to your account while you were gone.

ROBUX is the in-game currency. It's used to purchase new items for your character, new items for the game or anything else that's offered in the store. ROBUX can be earned or purchased through the store. This tab provides you with the shortcut to do so.

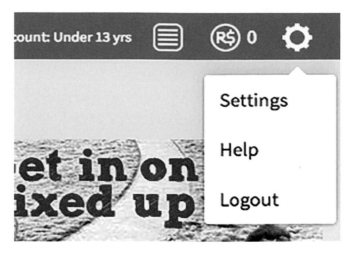

Changing the settings, getting help or logging out is done on the GEAR up in the top right-hand corner. Typing in questions for help is also possible from this button, just click on it to manage much of your account.

You must have a parent put their email into the setting section. They will need to confirm that you're able to play Roblox before the games can begin for real. Many features are disabled until after verification, so make sure to ask your parent to click the confirmation link that is sent to their email to help you get started as soon as possible.

Account Info, Security Settings, Privacy and Billing. All of these can be moderated through an adult that is connected to the Roblox account.

Once you've gone through the signup process, you can customize your character, play in the worlds that are already there or build your own world. Take a minute to familiarize yourself with some of the options available in the drop down menu to the left. You have options allowing you to customize your character, chat with friends, add new friends, use the forum and much more.

Home: Home is where you'd go to find the worlds and your general feed of news and other information.

Profile: Change your profile settings, name, birthday and email information.

Messages: Chat with your friends in the messages section. You can create your own message, receive them or look at them.

Friends: Keep track of all your friends in this area. This is where you can see if they're on and where they're currently playing.

Avatar: Change the look of your avatar when in this section. You can change skin, hair and clothes to best show off how you really look.

Inventory: Find the items that you have on your avatar for your game, as well as those items you've created on your own in this section.

Trade: You can trade with other members in Roblox. Easily find items you've traded and received through trades in this section.

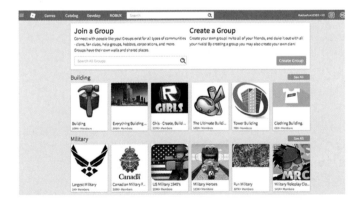

Groups: Create your own group, which is more like a club of friends, or join an existing one. Browse through active clubs until you find the one that's right for you.

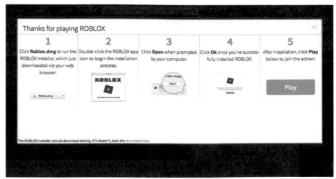

Forum: Ask questions, create your own thread or read what others are posting. If you're trying to make something in the game, this is the best place to go to find people that can give you more direction.

Blog: The blog is updated by the makers of Roblox every week. Learn more about what is changing, being added or taken away or just general Roblox news. Check here often for information related to the latest worlds.

Shop: Be directed to Roblox's Amazon store to purchase merchandise or in-game purchases to use during game play. A parent will have to purchase the items using their credit card, so always ask before making any purchases.

DOWNLOAD THE GAME

In order to play the game, you have to download the Roblox player to your computer. This is a simple task you can go through when you go to choose one of the games to play.

If you've not downloaded the player, you'll have a pop-up that tells you to download the game prior to playing. This can be done right from your computer and once complete, you can play the many different worlds whenever you'd like.

Click on the pop up to download the game to your computer. This should automatically start the download to your web browser.

Once it has downloaded, you can install it to your computer. Just click on the download file and open it up and click run or double click.

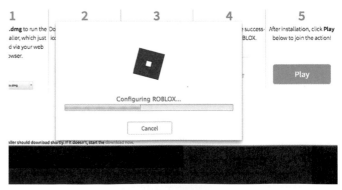

Once installed, it will then configure on your system so that it's able to run properly. This will take a few moments, so try to be patient while waiting to start gaming.

	Level	Kills
RobloxFun12333 Account: <13	1	0
Guest 6212	70	2,787
Hanson1230	59	2,312
mymythegreatestever	21	415
victorstop	4	68
rayashley	2	30
chadryeng	1	0
RobloxFun12333	1	0
smartpebble10	1	17

Time Left: 50

[rayashley]: hahahahahahahahah
[rayashley]: money y
Chat '/?' or '/help' for a list of chat commands.
[chadryeng]: omg

Hanson1230
chadryeng

RobloxFun12333 (100%)

Wave 1 | Survivors Left: 4
Level: 1

The game you've been wanting to try out is now playable. You just have to click on PLAY and then wait a moment. Click on yes, when it asks if you want to load the game. Then the game will begin.

Once the game loads, you'll see the welcome screen and the beginning of the game you chose. This is a user-created world that you're visiting. Feel free to explore your new surroundings, and most importantly, have fun!

Above is an example of a zombie hunting game. In it you have a team, and you must work together to kill off the zombies. You can chat up in the left hand corner with all the in-game players, creating a fun community aspect.

Are you ready to get started? Pick a game that looks interesting and give it a try!

WHAT

ROBLOX IS

Play
Stop
Test

Explorer

Filter workspace (Ctrl+Shift+X)

▶ Workspace
Players
DefaultToolboxSearch
▶ Lighting
ReplicatedFirst
ReplicatedStorage
ServerScriptService
ServerStorage
StarterGui
StarterPack
▶ StarterPlayer
Teams
SoundService
Chat

Properties

Filter Properties (Ctrl+Shift+P)

Learn more about Roblox and why you should play it!

Games   Catalog   Develop   ROBUX   Search 🔍   RobloxFun12333: <13   0

ROBLOX

JOIN THE #1 USER-GENERATED GAMING COMMUNITY

Our FREE platform enables anyone to push the limits of their imagination by creating immersive 3D multiplayer games and easily publish them to millions of players.

Open ROBLOX Studio

Continue to Develop page

All-In-One Development Engine

Our best-in-class authoring environment allows creators to build immersive 3D cross-platform games and launch them simultaneously on PC, Mac, iOS and Android devices, Xbox One and Oculus Rift.

- Built-in multiplayer and monetization tools
- One-click publishing
- Free cloud hosting
- Robust asset library

Reach Millions of Players

Connect with a massive audience by tapping into an incredibly enthusiastic and international community of over 28 million monthly players.

Chat & Party

WHAT ROBLOX IS

Roblox is an advanced tool and a game all in one. It allows you to be in charge of a custom character, and to create worlds where you can decide on themes, build empires and create your own rules. With this easy to use platform, you have everything you need to be in control.

Created for kids like you to enjoy, Roblox gives full control to the user behind the keyboard. Play with friends, play on your own, play with other kids on the other side of the planet, anything is possible with Roblox! You can play and create exactly the way you want, and make the game that you've always wanted to play!

Be the creator of a welcoming world open to all, or forge your own group that you're the proud leader of. You're the boss, you're the visionary, you're the ruler of your own world. Run it any way that you want to.

Learn more about Roblox, the worlds it offers and all the endless possibilities available in each and every one of them. You're an explorer, go out and explore!

A WORLD FULL OF WORLDS

Roblox features many different user-created worlds, and, you can choose to play one of those or make your own. The worlds allow you to connect with different people, play a variety of games and have fun while being creative and letting your imagination go free.

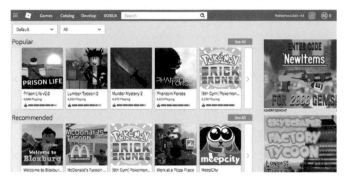

Choose Games found at the top left hand side.

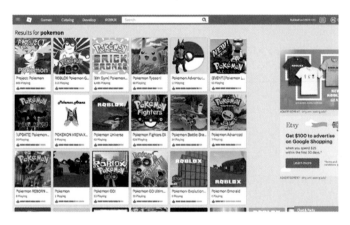

If you have a specific type of game in mind you'd like to play, it's easy to find it using search, just use the 'search' field at the top of the Home screen.

For example: a quick search for the term "Pokemon" brings up a long list of Pokemon-themed worlds to play in. A quick search makes it obvious just how easy it is to find a world that matches your interests. These are all user-created worlds that you can play with others, and you can access them with a single quick keyword.

You can search for just about any world that you can think of. You can also look through the most popular games being played at the time, or sort your options based on top rating, most recommended or features games. By scrolling through the options provided on the screen, you can find the world that speaks to you.

By entering one of these games, you can get into the action, but be prepared to follow the creator's rules. You can chat with the other players and have a great time.

Remember, you can also create your own world to be featured in one of the sections for others to come and visit!

TYPES OF WORLDS

You'll quickly see that there are many different types of worlds within the game, and it's up to you to decide on the one that best fits your interests.

Some of the more common types of worlds that can be found throughout Roblox are:

- Role Playing Games – Store, House, Work, Prison

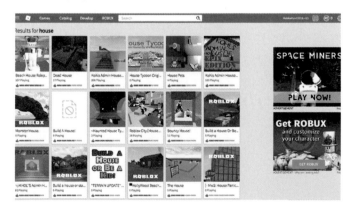

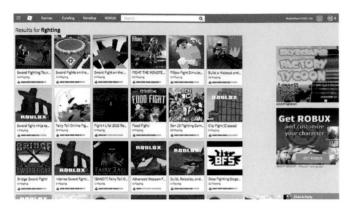

- **Action Games:** Shooting, Fighting, Capture the Flag

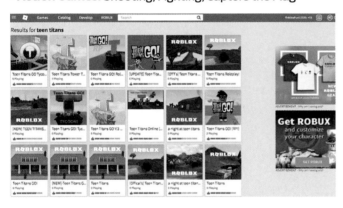

- **Building Games:** Carry out Interesting Construction Projects Within Someone Else's World
- **Visiting Games:** Just Enjoy the Experience Offered within the Game
- **Themed Games:** After Common Characters You Know, Pokemon, McDonald's, Teen Titans
- **Sports Games:** Dodgeball, Football, Soccer, Basketball
- **Racing Games:** Cars, Trucks, Monster Trucks, Classic Cars
- **Theme Parks, Zoos, Pizza Places and More!**

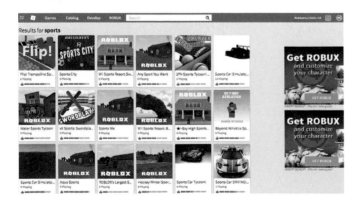

Just keep in mind that there are thousands upon thousands of games being offered. Thousands of other kids just like you have created their own worlds for others to join in on. You can make your own, as well.

It might be hard to choose just one to go with, but with so many options, you're sure to see something you like. Switch between them to find out what each has to offer and which you like the most. Exploring all the worlds is one of the most enjoyable aspects of Roblox, so test out a bunch!

THE DIFFERENCE BETWEEN SCRIPTING, MINI-WORLDS AND WORLDS

There's a big difference between the three main world types in Roblox — Scripted, Full Worlds and Mini Worlds. Each one of these is something different for the user to know. Understanding what each is while playing can give you a better idea of which you should be using for the specific game or task you'd like to do.

Scripting Worlds: Scripting is used to enhance worlds, create custom items and breathe life into the different objects throughout the Roblox universe. All the item functions, as well as some of their looks is controlled by scripting. Learning how to do it will give you more control when crafting your own worlds.

The programming language that is used for this scripting is Lua. It's a powerful tool that you can use to develop more in-depth items, worlds and game play. Using this language provides you with a way to create a full on, interactive game of your own, and it's the way that some of the coolest worlds in the game are made.

People have scripting worlds open for all that want to come and add items to them. These worlds give you the chance to try out some new items you made, build on something as a team and get pointers from other players that know how to use the scripting language.

This is highly recommended for new players that want to learn more about creating their own items and worlds through scripting.

Scripting provides the user with more abilities than just using stock items in RobloxStudio, but you'll have to learn more on how to use the language. You can learn more about this later on.

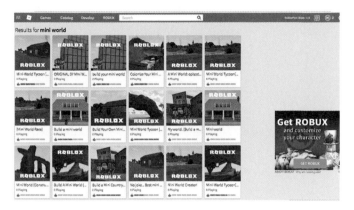

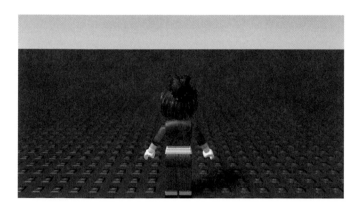

Worlds: Worlds are games that users create throughout the Roblox website. You can choose one of these to play in if you want to interact with others. They have a full interface with an objective you need to fulfill. This objective could be anything from cashing out a certain amount of customers to beating the other team by capturing their flag. The worlds in Roblox are limitless.

Full worlds are more advanced and have a lot more inside them. They might also have a common theme, a game to play or just an impressive landscape with buildings, islands, vehicles and other things for you to make use of.

These worlds are the most common places found throughout Roblox, and the most common thing players create. However, if you do not complete a whole world and make the world public for all to play, then you'd have a 'mini-world.'

Mini Worlds: Mini worlds can be visited but don't go into depth as much. They usually are user-created worlds that are not finished or that don't have much of an objective.

Users create them to allow other players to add to them, or as a place to go to practice building in some way when you're new to the game. They're also good tools for new players that want to be more creative.

Mini worlds sometimes provide small objectives, such as racing other players or building a few specific items. There are even worlds where you can learn how to build your own mini worlds.

The options on Roblox worlds, mini or not are expansive. If you can think something up, it has probably been created on Roblox. If you can't find what you're looking for with one of these three options, you can make one for others searching for the same type of thing, whether it's through advanced scripting, in a mini world or a full world, the option is all yours.

Any of the three types of worlds that you choose provide a fun experience, and each enriches Roblox just a bit more. It's important to note that you can use the RobloxStudio to create both the world and the mini world that you'd like to have on the website.

Now that you know about the different world types, it's time to dig into actual world options themselves. Knowing more about where you can go play is also a good thing. In the next chapter, you'll learn about some of the most highly featured, loved games found in Roblox. Find a world you'd like to try out or create one of your own!

TO GO PLAY

Filter workspa
- ▶ Works
- Player
- Lighting
- ReplicatedFirst
- ReplicatedStorage
- ServerScriptService
- ServerStorage
- StarterGui
- StarterPack
- ▶ StarterPlayer
- SoundService
- Chat
- HttpService
- InsertService

Properties

Filter Properties (Ctrl+Shift+P)

Many worlds and games are some of the best-rated by users, like you, check them out here!

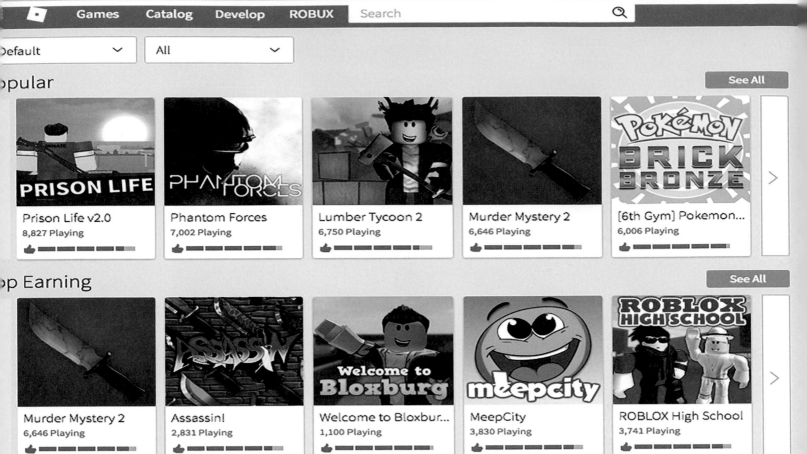

WHERE TO GO PLAY

With so many available worlds being offered, it's hard to choose where you might want to play. Some of the highest rated and loved games are listed below. Choose a world that fits you and what you want when you're ready to play and have fun.

Each of these worlds has been highly rated by not only regular players but some of the top players of the game. They're listed here so you can check them out for yourself and see if they have something appealing to you.

Of course, you can make your own creation as well, and make it just the way you want.

HIGHLY RATED ROBLOX GAMES

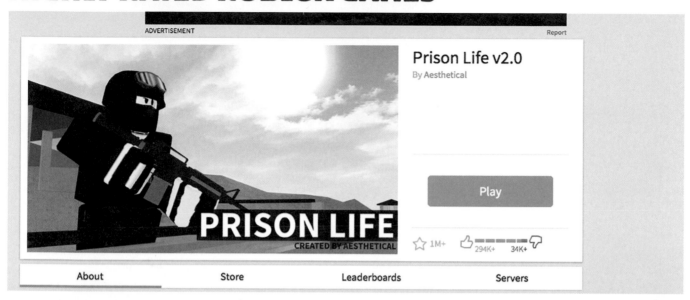

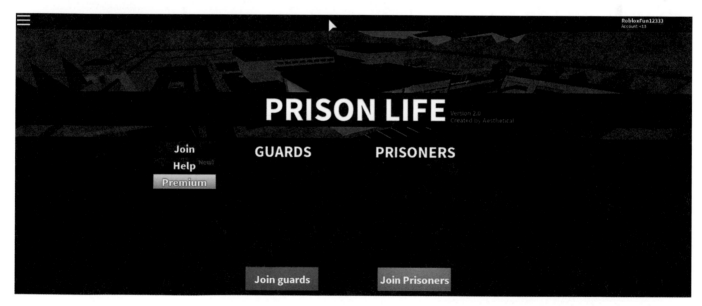

Prison Life v.2.0

This is one of the best Roblox games that you're likely to come across. It's packed with cool objectives, has a story behind it and is a whole lot of fun to play. You'll create your own story as a prisoner within one of the toughest prisons on Roblox, or perhaps you'll work as a guard trying to keep the prisoners in line.

As a guard, you'll be charged with protecting the prison and keeping prisoners from escaping the confinements they're supposed to be in. Work together with other players to meet your objective, whether it's keeping the prisoners locked away, or busting yourself out. More than 294,000 players have given the game a thumbs up, making it a highly rated and recommended game for all new players.

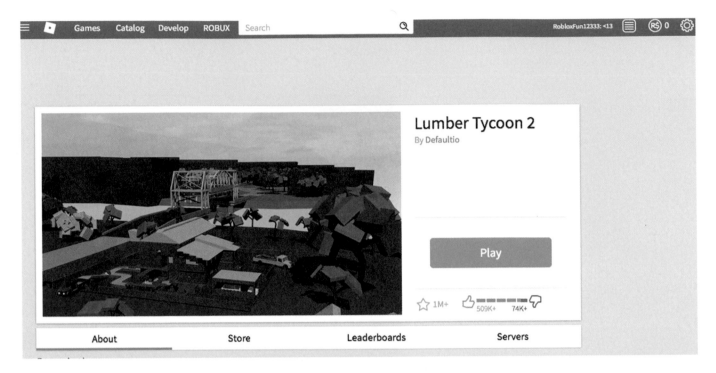

Lumber Tycoon 2

You're the lumberjack in this game. Grab an ax and find some trees that need to be cut down. The best lumberjack is the one that's able to bundle up the most trees and bring them back to the store to trade them for cold hard cash.

Rated as one of the best games by 509,000+ players, it's on the top featured games list for those looking for an exciting and rewarding game to play while on Roblox.

Murder Mystery 2

Excitement is what this game is all about. There are three different modes that you can choose when you enter into the game. Choose between a casual or 'normal' game play experience at the start. The hardcore choice starts you off without allies and no information at all. You'll be placed with likeminded players and you'll have to survive. Everyone has a knife and must fight for their survival.

Choosing casual or the 'normal' game play provides you with a way to get in the game and be the person that must solve the mystery, be an innocent person trying to get away from the murderer, or be the murderer. Everyone's role is determined at random by the computer.

With 549,000+ players that love this game and rated it a thumbs up, it's definitely worth checking out for yourself to see how you like it.

These are just the top choices for the featured games that Roblox offers. In the next chapter, we'll discuss some of the top Roblox world creators, groups that you can become a part of and the worlds that they've put together.

MASTER BUILDER ROBLOX

ALL THE

Defau...

Popular

Prison Life v2.0

14,052 Playing

[2v2 Battles] Pokem...

11,255 Playing

Epic Minigames

11,190 Playing

Murder Mystery 2

11,034 Playing

610,727   47,784

By Nikilis

Phantom For...

10,023 Playing

Top Earning

Murder Mystery 2

11,184 Playing

Assassin!

5,777 Playing

Welcome to Bloxbur...

2,152 Playing

ROBLOX High School

4,495 Playing

[2v2 Battles] ...

11,364 Playing

Top Rated

ROBLOX GAMES TO PLAY

See All

Lumber Tycoon 2
7,748 Playing

See All

MeepCity [EASTER S...
5,748 Playing

See All

Zombie Rush

Find out what games are the most popular and where you should go to play!

list of chat commands.

The lances will stop striking in 49 seconds; avoid being skewed

RobloxFun12333
Account: <13

Guest 8132

SUPERMANJUELA

EVBRI09

dhggcnc

ninjaerde

hdgameytb

denisgirl125

Guest 5363

megan1810

RobloxFun12333

Seasoned

ALL THE ROBLOX GAMES TO PLAY AND WHO'S MAKING THEM

There are many different Roblox games available today. Choosing which one to play can be tough, but knowing what you like might make it a little simpler. By playing a few of the games that are offered, you can learn more about what you like and dislike, and narrow down the type of games that you want to play. Hopefully this will lead to having a lot of fun in the worlds.

Because there's so many different players and creators, there's a huge library of games to choose from. This is what makes Roblox unique from all other gaming experiences, and it's why it's worth trying out.

Not only are the players different, the groups and games they make are as well. Roblox is a place where creativity rules. You can be anyone you want, play any game you want and open your worlds up to others out there with similar ideas.

You're in control when playing Roblox and you can create just about anything you can think of. Put your creativity to good use and find out what players, groups and games there are currently throughout the Roblox universe.

It's likely that you'll be inspired by some of them, and you could end up making the next top creation.

TOP PLAYERS

Many of the top players put out new games consistently, working hard to offer the very best experiences for other players. These top players have groups, specialized games and YouTube channels for you to visit to learn more about what they've done in the past.

By knowing some of these top players, you can find out what cool games they're able to offer you and what's coming next. Just friend them to keep on top of all that information.

Nikilis: Nikilis, one of the top ranking players in Roblox is behind the game Murder Mystery 2, a top game in the Roblox community. With over 350 million visits, the game has gotten a lot of attention. The server for the game is large, allowing thousands of people to play at once. There could be anywhere from 10,000 to 30,000 people playing at any one time, but worlds are limited to 12 at a time.

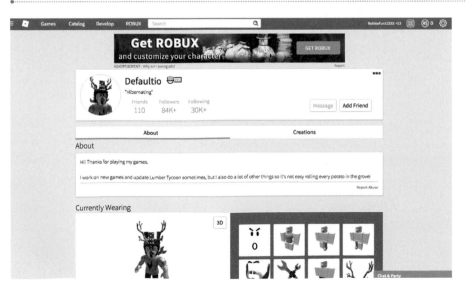

Defaultio: With over 84,000+ followers, Defaultio is a top ranking player that's gained ground in the Roblox community. Being the creator of a number of games, but the biggest being Lumber Tycoon and Lumber Tycoon 2, he's gained a lot of attention in those areas. Lumber Tycoon gets over 170 million visits, which made it steadily climb up the ladder and bring fame to this Roblox player. His other games have also gained traction due to the large fan base of the Lumber Tycoon games.

Cindering: With 114,000 followers and counting, Cindering is a big name within the Roblox community. He is also the winner of the 2015 BLOXY award for the Best Mobile Game. These awards are handed out each year to the players that do well. He is the creator of Roblox High School. With almost 300 million players visiting the game, he has made an impact in the community for sure.

Dued1: Dued1 is well known throughout the community due to Work at a Pizza Place and Pizza Place Mobile. Both worlds provide users with the chance to simulate working within a pizza shop. With close to 270 million visitors to the game, he has definitely made the top games and players list. With over 150,000 followers, he continues to provide value to a huge group of players with his exciting games.

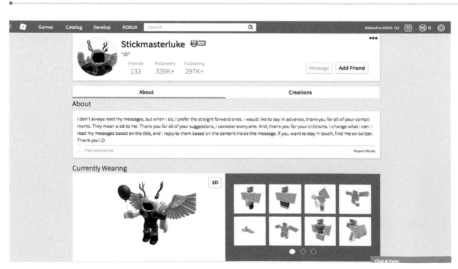

Stickmasterluke: One of the biggest names in the Roblox community, Stickmasterluke has close to 340,000 followers. He's brought games such as the Underground War with 20 million visitors, Cube Eat Cube and the biggest, Natural Disaster Survival with close to 260 million visitors. Each game continues to get better and better that come from Stickmasterluke.

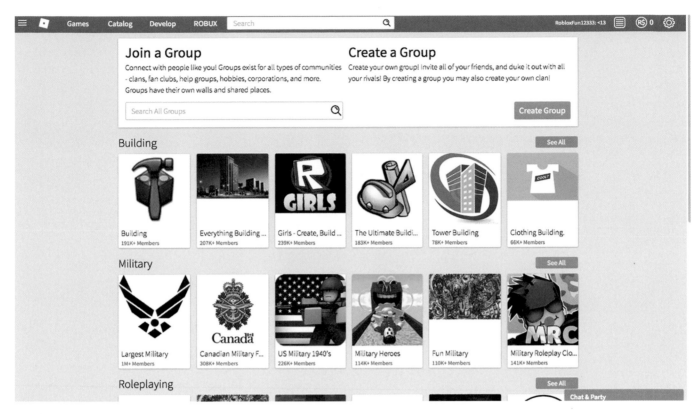

TOP GROUPS

In addition to players, there are also groups that can be found, joined or invited to within the community. These groups are generally filled with friends, both online and those that know each other, that go into the games as a team. These groups are much like clubs that you'd invite your friends to, so that you can do battles and other games with one another easily. There are super groups that have thousands of members within the organizations. These groups can usually be found inside many different games, but when there is a team match or fight, they tend to play together. **Here are some of the top named groups with the largest number of members among them.**

The Roblox Assault Team:

This is one of the largest groups that can be found within the Roblox community. With 212,000 members and counting, they're open to the public and allow anyone to come join their ranks. They have been found to win most of their games, but there is also a lot of talk about them not playing fair.

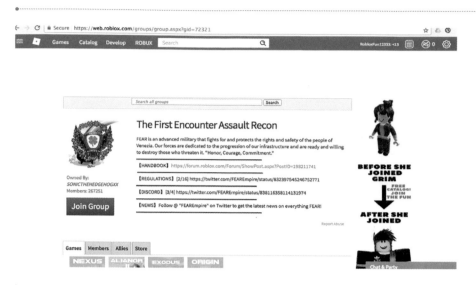

The First Encounter Assault Recon:
The First Encounter Assault Recon is another one of the biggest groups that can be found throughout the Roblox community. They have a bit more controversy over the games that they've won as compared to the group above. However, they've received a lot of recognition for the games that they've won fair. They have 267,000 members and are a private group. This means you must be invited to join them.

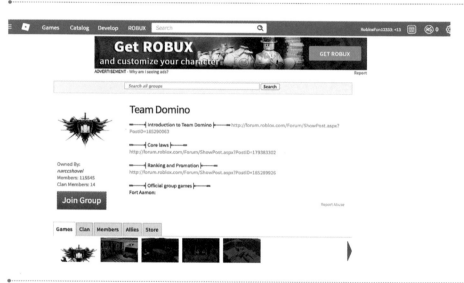

Team Domino:
Team Domino is not as large as the others, but it still has a sizeable community. The club has a public group that is open to anyone that wants to come and join their forces. With over 115,000 members, they're always looking for more community members. There's a wealth of information about the group provided for those that want to join up with them. They also welcome questions about the group and what they do.

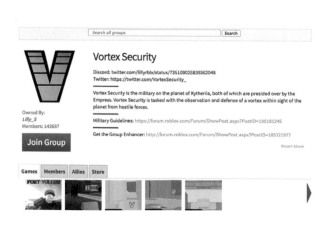

Vortex Security:
Bigger than the above group, but smaller than the others; Vortex Security provides a public group for anyone to join with. This is a tactical team that is looking to take over many of the games that they focus on. They have more information in the links that they provide on the group's page. With over 140,000 members and counting, they welcome those that want to be a part of their group.

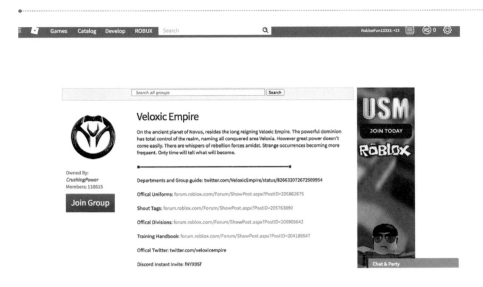

Veloxic Empire: With over 110,000 members in the group, you'll enjoy a thriving community and a welcome atmosphere at Veloxic Empire. Their team wears a specific uniform, while also providing information on joining the group. As a member you'll learn about team fights and matches that they have going on throughout the week as well. You can become a member by sending them a request to be added to the group.

Departments and Group guide: twitter.com/VeloxicEmpire/status/826632072672509954

Offical Uniforms: forum.roblox.com/Forum/ShowPost.aspx?PostID=205862675

Shout Tags: forum.roblox.com/Forum/ShowPost.aspx?PostID=205763890

Offical Divisions: forum.roblox.com/Forum/ShowPost.aspx?PostID=205905642

Training Handbook: forum.roblox.com/Forum/ShowPost.aspx?PostID=204189547

It's always good to read the information that these groups provide on their pages. It can provide you with more information regarding who they are, what they expect from you and how you can join with them.

Some groups prefer you to play a certain amount of hours, or have an account that is a specified amount of time old. You just have to find the group that works for you.

All of these groups are specialized in the tactical fighting games, which means you have to be comfortable playing these games to join up in the first place.

While they have a specialized area, it doesn't mean that other groups are the same. There are groups for other games as well, and you should be able to find a place you can join with other like-minded players. Some may play more of the role-playing games such as store, house or high school while others play the racing games.

Speaking with more players while playing the games can give you an idea of what types of groups are out there and who you want to join up with.

Remember, you can also create your own group if you're a Builder's Club Member!

WHAT'S A BUILDER'S CLUB MEMBER?

The Builder's Club is a club that is offered through Roblox. In order to join, you have to pay a monthly membership fee. This gives you access to exclusive areas that free members can't visit. The level of membership that you go with will give you less or more access, depending on what purchase you make.

Many of the bigger names in Roblox are Builder's Club members, because they rely on the extra resources that members get.

If you're serious about Roblox and playing, a Builder's Membership might be the right fit for you!

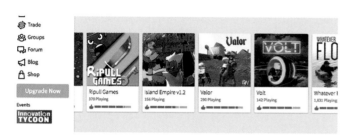

Going to UPGRADE in the lower left hand corner of the screen will bring you to where you can sign up for Builder's Club.

There are four options that you can choose from — Free, Classic, Turbo and Outrageous. How much access you want determines which level is the best for you to go with.

Each one of the tiers has a specific amount of 'extras' that you get when you sign up with the account. With all the paid memberships, you remove the ads, sell stuff, get a virtual hat, bonus gear, BC beta features and can use the trade system. You also have access to some of the tools, such as being able to create a group when you want for your friends.

You are limited to the amount that you can make while in the club, depending on your membership level. Classic only allows you to join and create up to 10 groups, Turbo allows up to 20 each and Outrageous gives you access to 100 groups you can join and create.

They provide sign on bonuses for those that sign up with one of the three clubs. You can get up to 100 ROBUX back for free, which you can use inside the stores to buy merchandise or gear for your character.

In order to sign up with the Builder's Club, you must have ROBUX in your account. These can be purchased from the ROBUX section on the left. A parent's credit card and authorization are required to pay for ROBUX that will be used to fund a membership and other purchases as well.

The prices range from $5.95 to $19.95 per month, or you can pay annually for the membership. Monthly memberships auto-renew each month, so the credit card on file is going to be charged every month at the same time.

Ask a parent or guardian if you can sign up for the Builder's Club or just enjoy all the free features that come with the game!

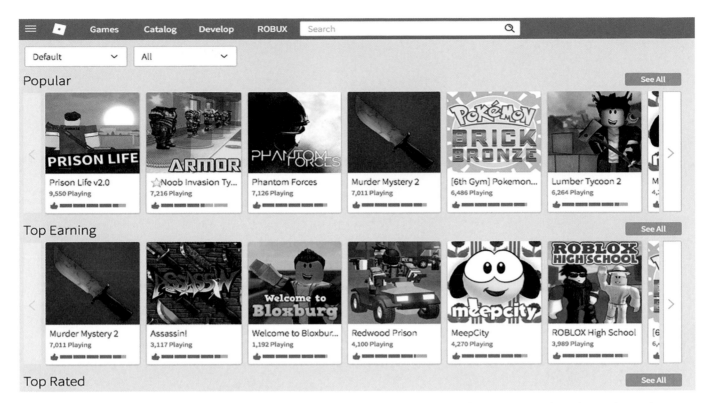

FEATURED GAMES

There are many featured games you can play within Roblox. The games don't stop there though. You can go to almost any game you can think of with help from the search bar, and you can find it in a matter of seconds.

The search bar gives you fast access to every single game you want to play. Each of the worlds and mini worlds within the game are all on the website.

You just have to make sure you put the right words into the search bar for the game you're thinking of playing. Putting in Pokemon, House, Pizza, Hospital and so on will bring you to the games that are closely related to the word you put in.

Here are some of the top featured games that you can play when it comes to having a little fun while in Roblox! You can try them out for yourself to see if they have what you need when it comes to finding something fun to do!

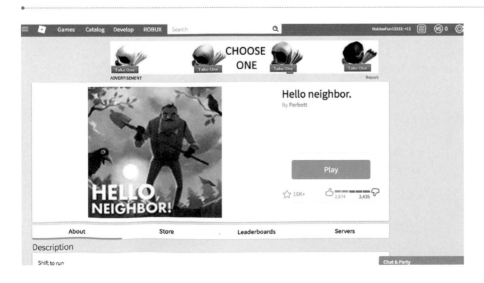

Hello Neighbor!: Hello Neighbor is a fascinating game fast becoming a hit on Roblox. You start out in your home and have to run across the street to the neighbor's. It's up to you to find the basement door and go down before the neighbor notices that you're in their house. It's definitely a game that will get your blood pumping. It's exciting and you'll spend a lot of time trying to be the winner. **Made by tristansew**

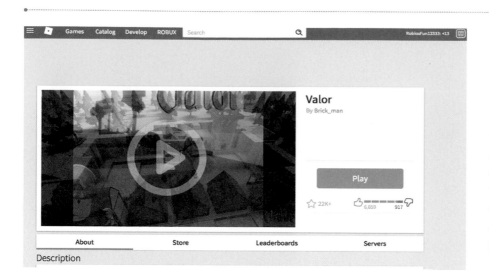

Valor: This game is fast paced and set in medieval times, allowing you to be the knight in shining armor. A group of 6 will be fighting the attacker, who is chosen at random when entering into the game. The attacker must come up with a strategy to beat the six players that are trying to stop him (or her) from taking over the town they're all in. It's exciting and forces you to think strategically.
Made by Brick_man

Volt: Volt was nominated for the BLOXY's, since it is one of the most loved games that can be found in Roblox. Based on Disney's TRON, they have many different objectives for you to play out while inside the game. Compete against others as a team or a single and fight for your life. If you get off the trail or leave the arena, then you're out of the game. You'll have to wait for the next round and start over.
Made by TeamVolt

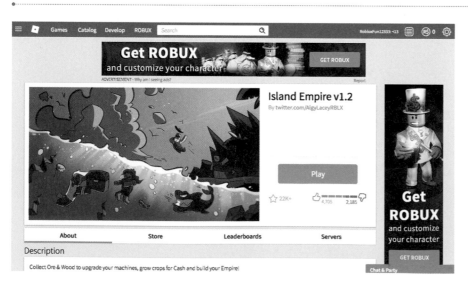

Island Empire: Build your empire by getting crops, cash, ore and wood. Grow the machines that you have, as well as your land to win. The more you do, the more you can grow the empire that you call your own. If you complete the missions that are given to you, you can unlock new pets, items and get promotions to move up ranks. This game gives you a range of objectives to conquer, and you'll have fun creating brand-new machines.
Made by twitter.com/AlgyLaceyRBLX

Roblox Titanic: You must find ways to solve problems, save other passengers on the boat, as well as yourself. You get boats for all the problems that you solve and people that you save. The boat will go under within a specified amount of time, so you must race the clock to do everything in your power to save everyone off the ship in time, including yourself! Good luck!

Made by Virtual Valley Games

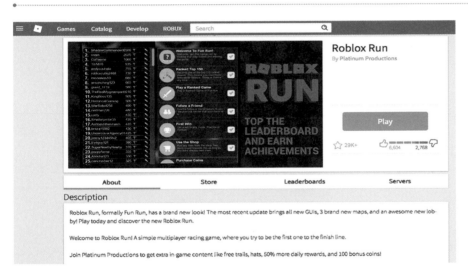

Roblox Run: Roblox Run was once known as Fun Run. You go into game play as a racer and have to try to beat the other players that are in the game. You run as your person to the finish line and must navigate the track. Some of the courses put obstacles in your way that you have to find ways to get over or around. It is fast paced and you get points for winning the game.

Made by Platinum Productions

Whatever Floats Your Boat: This game allows players to use their imaginations to create a boat. The boat must be tested in the water and you can use any of the props that are lying around or bring your own. You have to go against the other players to see who's boat is actually going to make it out on the waters. This is a game where anything goes, which makes it all the more exciting when it's time to play.

Made by Quenty

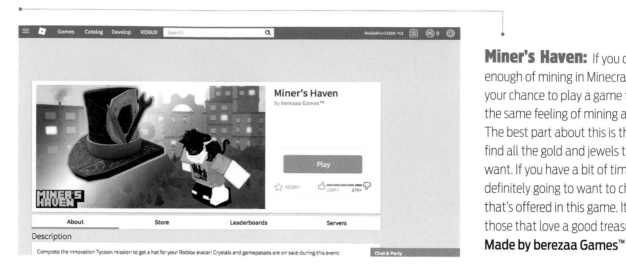

Miner's Haven: If you didn't get enough of mining in Minecraft, now is your chance to play a game that mimics the same feeling of mining and building. The best part about this is that you can find all the gold and jewels that you want. If you have a bit of time, then you're definitely going to want to check out all that's offered in this game. It's made for those that love a good treasure hunt. **Made by berezaa Games™**

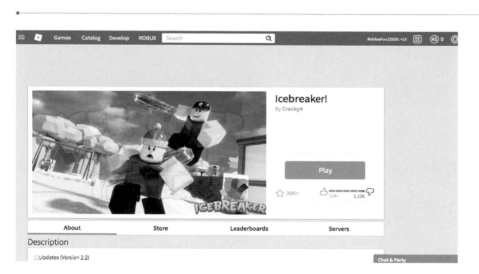

Icebreaker: Icebreaker is an exciting, fast paced game that welcomes everyone to come out and try their luck. You're on a team and have to go around freezing enemies, then unfreezing teammates that have been caught. It's a quick paced, quirky game of tag that you can play completely on your screen, which makes it a great way to get out there and have some fun.

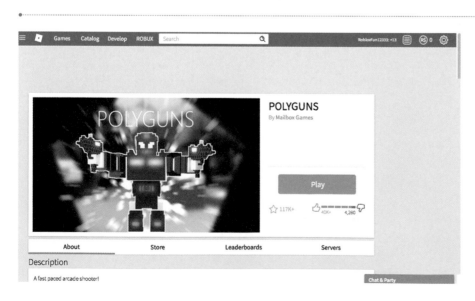

Polyguns: You're a robot that's trying to race against time and take out the other team. Outfitted with some of the coolest guns out there, you can run across the field and take out the enemy. Make sure to come up with a game strategy and then try your best to rack up as many points as possible before the game ends. Modeled after arcade games, it provides an exciting way to take on other players in a fun gun battle. **Made by Mailbox Games**

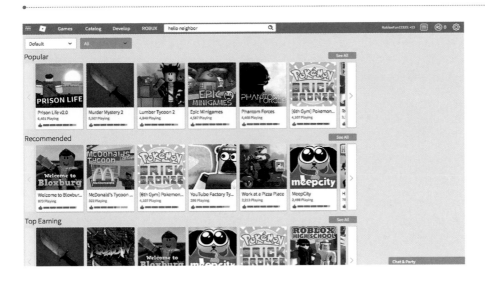

It doesn't matter which game you choose to play. There are literally thousands to choose from on Roblox, and you can even create a specific game that you're interested in. It's up to you to find exactly what you're looking for and have a great time on this top-notch online game.

Remember, you can find the featured, top rated, popular, recommended and top earning games right in the games section of the page. You just scroll down to find the different sections of games offered and choose the type of games that sound the best to you.

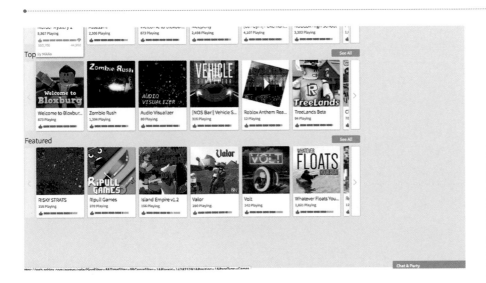

You just have to scroll to the bottom for the featured games. Use the arrows on the right and left to scroll through the many options that they have available for you to use.

You can also use the drop-down menu to track down Top Earning, Recommended or Top Featured games. It starts off set to Default, but you can change it to another category that you would rather see. Just pull it down and switch to one of the other lists to see games you are most interested in.

ADDING GAMES TO YOUR FAVORITES MENU

When you find a game that you really love, add it to the Favorites section of your page so you can find it again easily the next time you want to play.

On the top left hand side, you will notice a drop-down menu. It's automatically put into the Default mode to show you the top-ranking games, as well as featured games. You can skip this portion if you already have some games saved to the Favorites section of your home page.

Pull down the menu where it says Default and then click on My Favorite. This is where you'll be able to find all the games that you favorited.

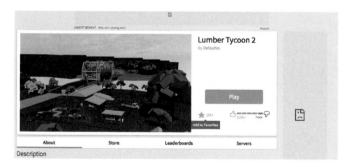

If you're unsure of how to Favorite a game, you just have to go to the specific game that you want to add to the favorites. After setting a few games to favorites, I was amazed at how easy it was to get them started the next time I wanted to play.

The star that is below the PLAY button in the home page of the game screen is where you favorite the game. This places it into the Favorite menu, so you can quickly jump to that area when you want to play a game that you liked the first time around.

Lumber Tycoon 2
By Defaultio

Play

⭐ 1M+   👍 510K+ ▬▬▬▬ 74K+ 👎

YOU CAN RATE GAMES

Rating the games can also be beneficial not only to the game makers, but to other players that were thinking about playing the games. By seeing how many liked and disliked the game, they have a better idea of whether or not they want to play it.

Rating games is easy. After you get done playing the game, you just have to click on the thumbs up or thumbs down buttons that are provided under the PLAY section. This will boost the rating or lower the rating, depending on the score you give it. This is a good way to find out if a game works how it should and provides you with the game play you'd expect or not, and how detailed the game really is.

When you create your own game, you'll find that people do the same for you!

If you're curious about what each of the games is about before playing them, the ABOUT section below the picture and PLAY button provides a little more information about the game and what is expected from you when you go in to play it. However, this is just a quick snippet and you're not going to know what to expect until you actually play the game for yourself. So get in there and check it out!

Learn more about making something yourself in the next chapters! You'll be able to create a world that's all your own once you learn more about the RobloxStudio.

About	Store	Leaderboards	Servers

Description

Got a cool base? Tweet me a picture! twitter.com/Defaultio

Check the changelog to keep up with the most recent updates. You can find it in the game menu.

There are lots of physics bugs in this game. Some of them I can try to fix, and some of them are out of my control. I am trying to distinguish between those. Please send me as detailed bug reports as you can when you do come across them.

Visits	Created	Updated	Max Players	Genre	Allowed Gear types
170M+	7/31/2009	3/11/2017	6	Adventure	[×]

This game is copylocked

Report Abuse

MASTER BUILDER ROBLOX

MAKING

This game is currently the #1 most favorited game for the keyword

Make a Cake Recipe Book.

This Recipe Book is used to make certain kinds of cakes, using different choices for oven temperature, frosting, and toppings. All recipies are optional, with actually over 300 cake combinations.

Next

Close

Teleport to VIP

Teleport to Shop

Teleport to Museum

Teleport to Spawn

Teleport to Noob

Teleport to Bonus Room

Teleport to Mini Obby

Teleport to Control Room

Chocolate Cake - 150

De-Cakifyer

This game is made by thebenster

Cake Recipe Book

Edible Batter

SOMETHING YOURSELF

ke and candy!

florjula 40

Guest 9252 40

RobloxFun12333 40

1amJam012 15

upcake (One Use) - 50

Don't just play the games and worlds, create your own for others to play!

MAKING SOMETHING YOURSELF

Making something yourself is a great way to start in the world of Roblox. The entire game is built on a series of games that players (like you) have created. You can be the person that goes to each of these games, or you can make your own to put out there for others to play.

Your options are limitless when it comes to what you can and cannot create, but you want to make sure that you're able to provide an epic world that everyone is going to love. Who knows, your world might even be voted to receive the BLOXY award for the upcoming year.

Check out some of the ways that you can make something to get started. You'll need to have RobloxStudio downloaded and installed to your computer. This should have been done when the game player was installed. Instead of a red square, the RobloxStudio is a blue one.

Are you ready to make something for yourself?

MAKING AN EPIC WORLD

Want to create a world of your own? Want it to be home to massive duels between witches and wizards? Or would you rather be a pirate capturing ships in deadly waters filled with other players? How about just a place for you and your friends to chill? You can make a world where you're able to do almost anything.

Making your own epic world is just a few steps away. Invite whoever you want and even open your brand-new world to the general public to meet awesome new people looking for a fun new experience.

Starting with the controls and being able to go from there when it comes to creating is a great way to learn and start slow. Before you know it, you'll be a regular at creating your own worlds, gear and other items.

You must sign into the studio to use it. This can be done in the right-hand corner. It will ask you to sign up or sign in. I signed in with my screen name and the editor was quickly ready to go.

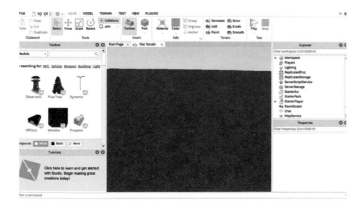

Focusing the Camera: Roblox features a free-floating camera allowing you and other players to see the world from any view that you'd like. This is true for Studio mode as well, which helps with making those important edits and placing objects in your world.

Roblox features a free-floating camera in the Studio, making it easy to see all the edges of your budding world, but you can choose the perspective players see when they join your game. Decide how you and others will see your world, and bring your game to life!

You just have to right click on the screen and drag it around to get the camera to the desired angle.

Making Use of Key Commands:

W and S - Forwards and Backwards

A and D - Side to Side

E and Q - Up and Down

Holding SHIFT down while rotating the camera makes it move slower

, and . - Rotates the camera in place

Page Up and Page Down - Pitches the camera up or down

F - Focuses the camera on one particular object that is selected, use the rotation controls to move the camera in this view or one of the movement keys to get out of Focus.

If you've already played Roblox, the Studio comes right with the game, so you have everything you need to create your own worlds from the very beginning. To open up the studio, simply press the START Windows key and look under the same menu that the Roblox client is located. You'll see a Studio application icon, select that and start creating your own world straight out of your imagination.

Choose a Terrain to go with on the START page of the editor. You can choose from a few different options - Baseplate, Flat Terrain, Castle, Village, Suburban, Racing, Western and so on. Choose which one closely relates to the game you're trying to make.

ROBLOX

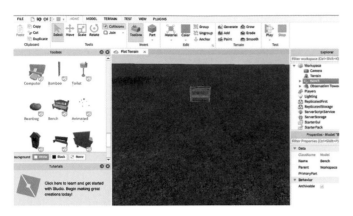

I decided to go with Flat Terrain. It's a blank canvas for you to add to. On the left-hand side, there are plenty of objects and furniture, as well as outdoor items that you can use to furnish and build your world. The user of the items is listed, but they're free for everyone to use within their own worlds.

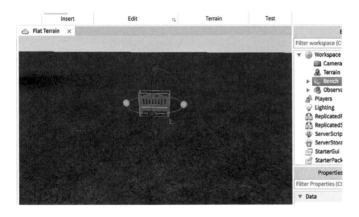

I chose to place a bench down. When placing it down, it was facing the wrong way. Up in the left-hand side on the editor, clicking ROTATE easily turns the item around. You're given a sphere and you drag the colored circles to get the item in the desired location.

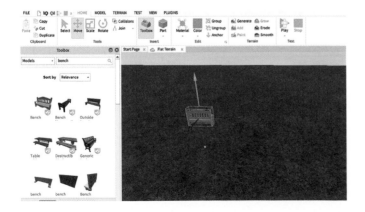

Everything is in the right scale when it's added to your world. You can move items by clicking the MOVE button up at the top of the editor, as well as change their scale to size them correctly with the world you're building.

Follow this same process throughout the rest of the creation process to create a whole world that is dedicated to the specific theme that you want.

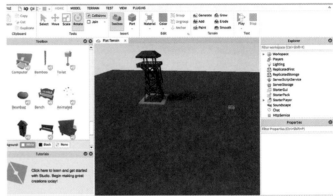

You can also create your own items by using parts. If something that you need is not found in the toolbox of items, you can easily search for the specific items. All you'd have to do is click on PART up in the editor section.

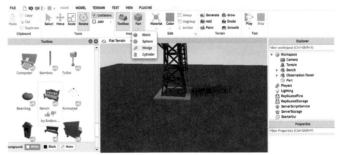

A part is then automatically added to the screen. You can choose from a block, sphere, wedge or cylinder to get the correct shape for the item that you want to build.

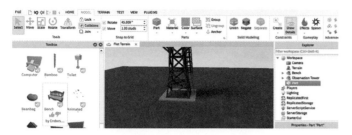

Once the item is in place, you can begin molding it to how you want it to look in the game. You must go to the model tab up at the top by terrain to edit the settings on the specific block that you're going to be making a part of your game.

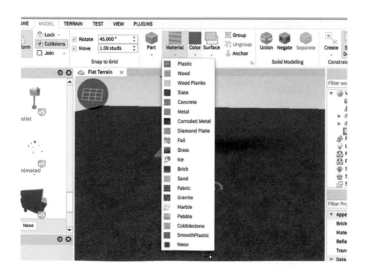

By using the top controls, you can make nearly any changes you want to the small part. By clicking on the material, color or surface, it gives the part a different look and feel to make it a part of the game.

The material button allows you to switch through different materials for your part, such as wood, metal, grass, brick, concrete, ice and so many others.

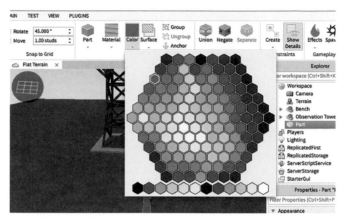

Choose the color that works with what you're trying to build. You can match the color to the type of material that you chose for the item. This will give it a great look!

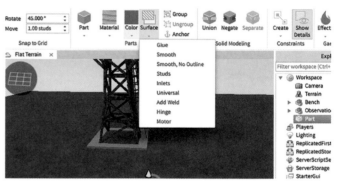

The surface can be smooth, jagged, edgy or whatever you want it to be, depending on what you're trying to make. With this option, you can change the overall look and feel of the part by just clicking which one works best with the item.

In the top left corner, you can choose from many other options that allow you to move, rotate, re-size and more. You can place the part wherever you'd like in the game or even flip it on its side, up against a wall or move it to another area. If you want the piece to be larger, you can rescale it to the size you're looking for.

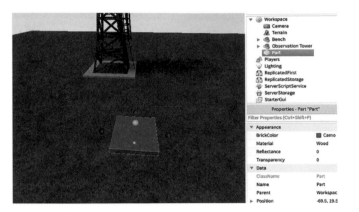

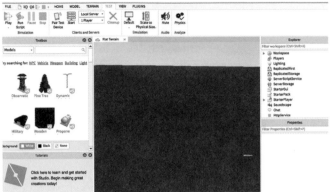

Finding Items in the Toolbox

Searching through the toolbox of items is easy, as well. If nothing is up front when you're building, you can look for the specific parts you're in need of right on the left-hand side.

There is a search bar available in this section. This provides you with a way to search up all the items within the toolbox. You just have to make sure that you put in the exact name of the item to find the right one. Some of them will come up when there is a word that is close to what you're looking for.

If you want to get a better search result, choosing the type of item you're searching for from the drop-down menu can help. This provides you with a way to get a more accurate search result. It's important to type in a relating term, otherwise you'll have trouble finding the item that you are looking for.

Once you've completed the world, you can test it before saving. Test it out on the top tab titled TEST. It's best to go to this tab and test out your world before making it public for other players to try out. You can click on RUN SCRIPT and the game will do a rundown of what it will look like for visitors that open it up for the very first time.

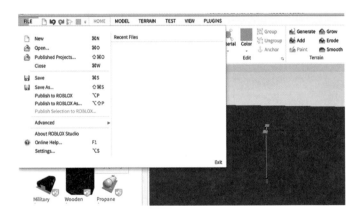

Once you're satisfied with the results, you should make sure to save the game, so you can release it to the public so they can give it a try. This can be done by going to FILE at the top left hand corner and clicking on Save. If you want to publish it for players to visit, you just have to click PUBLISH TO ROBLOX.

Scripting is something that can also be done within the game to make it more personable to the player that visits. With the scripts, you can add secret messages, put in more commands or make certain parts in the game more functional.

Lua is the language that is used to create scripting in Roblox. You can learn more about Lua in the next chapters. Using this language can help your game become much more involved and player-friendly.

ACCESSING YOUR OWN PLACE MODELS

If you've gotten place models through friends, games or other ways such as the store, you might want to add them into the world. You don't have to search through the inventory of the toolbox to do so.

You can access all your saved place models in one area in the toolbox.

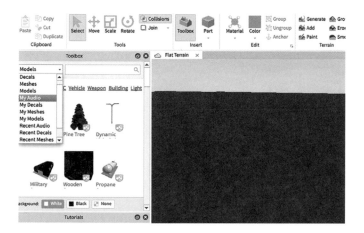

While in the editor section creating a world, you can use the drop-down menu to access all of the inventory you're going to need.

Just go down to MY MESHES, MY DECALS, MY AUDIO or whatever you want to use inside the game that you're currently building.

You can then click on which item you'd like to add and place it into the game.

CUSTOMIZING YOUR CHARACTER

Every Roblox player gets a character, and that character can be customized in depth. You'll have a wide range of customization options to get your guy or girl looking just the way you want. Roblox starts you off with a few of their own designs, but you can change through what is given or use what you purchase in the store with ROBUX or even create your own clothing in the editor.

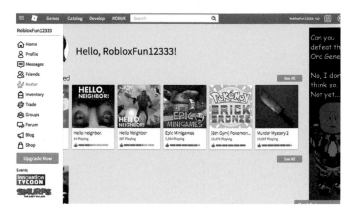

Go to Avatar in the drop-down menu on the left-hand side of the Home Screen to customize the avatar you have.

In this section, you'll find a variety of appearance options to switch through. You can do everything from changing hair and clothing to actual body parts. You're in control when it comes to how you want your avatar to look.

You can also change the color of the avatar using the sliding scales at the bottom of the screen. If you prefer to have an alien avatar, then green skin might be the best way to go!

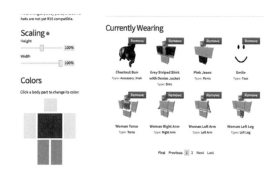

You can search through the many different accessories and parts of outfits that you have in your inventory at the top. In the accessories section, the drop-down menu shows you all of the accessories that are given based on where they're worn.

For example, on the neck would be a necklace. The face would be sunglasses and so on.

Avatar Customizer

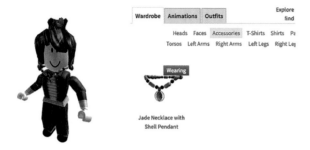

Jade Necklace with
Shell Pendant

You can add the item to the avatar by clicking WEAR.

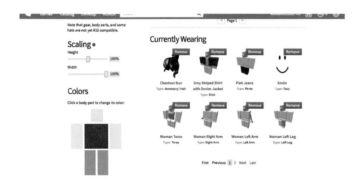

To remove the item, you just have to click on REMOVE in the bottom section of options for the avatar, and poof! They're gone.

MAKING A FORUM THREAD FOR CONNECTING WITH ALL

Chatting with friends using the in-game client is fun, but if you want to bring the conversation out of any one world and talk with an entire community that supports your game, you should consider launching a forum thread for your game on the official Roblox Forum.

This is an open-ended way to reach every player in the game, whether they're on the same world as you or not. A forum thread is also a great way for beginners to ask questions and get answers from those that have been playing the game longer.

Have a question? Just want to chat? Hook yourself up with a forum thread!

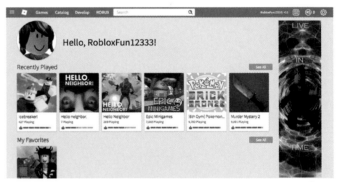

Go to Roblox.com — Sign in to your existing account with your Roblox username and password

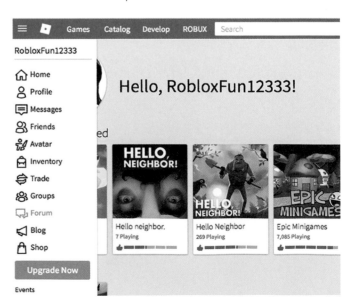

Click on the drop-down menu of pages that you can visit and go to the one that says FORUM

Select a subject that most closely relates to what you want to do in the forum. For example, if you're interested in showing off a world that you made, you can click on ROBLOX FUN — Each section explains what they are best used for. You just have to read the description to find out which one works for the subject matter you want to talk about.

Click the NEW THREAD button. This brings you to a page with a SUBJECT line and MESSAGE area.

Fill in the SUBJECT line with the subject that you want, ex: CHECK OUT THIS EPIC WORLD! Or HAVE A QUESTION ABOUT BUILDING?

Put your question or your world in the message section and give more information.

Click on PREVIEW to see your forum thread and if you like the way it looks, click on POST

Wait for responses on your thread and connect with new people!

There is also a HELP tab if you're having a bit of trouble creating a new thread and need additional information.

Also, if you're a new user and only have been for under 24 hours, you cannot create a forum thread just yet. Make sure your account is at least a day old and you shouldn't have any problems connecting with other players online.

Starting in the world of Roblox can be exciting and fascinating if you've never played it before. With the right help and practice, you can make some of the best games out there.

You can also advertise them, and even make money off the games you allow others to play. Once you're done creating some worlds and trying out others, becoming better at Lua and building worlds should become easier to do. From there, you can advertise the worlds and make some money off of them.

Learn even more about building your own world in the next chapters!

MASTER BUILDER ROBLOX

ROBLOX

Imperium

Imperium Peaceful Lands, Smaller map and feature restricted but you don't lose items or gold upon death. Recommended for new players.

Play

Play

Follow Friend

Player Name

Tutorial

Tournament

Start a tournament ser make participants folk you

STUDIO TABS

Start your world on this tab and create something worth showing off to other players!

Warring Kingdoms, ...assic Imperium ...Bigger map, badges ...vements. You lose ...d gold upon death.

ROBLOX STUDIO TABS: HOME

RobloxStudio is a tool with many tabs to choose from up top. In order to effectively create a world of your own, you have to know what each of them is, and what they do.

When you go through the options, you'll find that each tab has a different use, giving you just the tools you need to create something in your world. Each one provides you with a way to change the overall look or actions associated with game play.

Here, you will learn what to expect with the HOME tab at the top of the RobloxStudio.

This is the first tab out of six that are at the top of the Studio. Learn what all of the functions can do for you and make sure to test your game out as you go along!

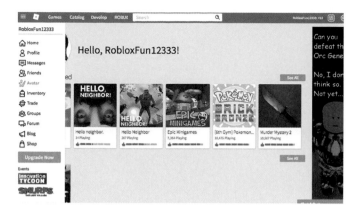

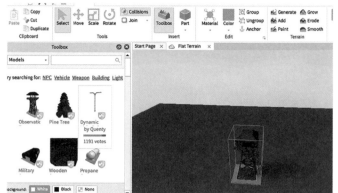

HOME: When entering into the game, you start at the HOME tab, so there is no need to worry about switching to the right one.

Click on an item from the toolbox to use these tools on it to customize the world however you'd like.

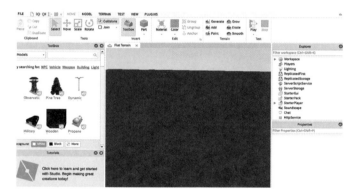

ACTION	DESCRIPTION
PASTE	Put down a copy of an item that was previously copied with this tool.
COPY	Save a copy of an object to your clipboard to use later on with the paste function.
CUT	Remove an item from your world while copying it to the clipboard at the same time. You can paste it back in later on.
DUPLICATE	Copy an existing object without erasing it. You can easily paste the object down once again in a differnet location.

Start the editing process by choosing a template. This opens up access to the rest of the tools located in the HOME tab.

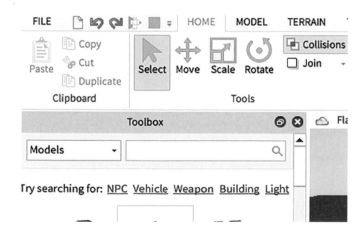

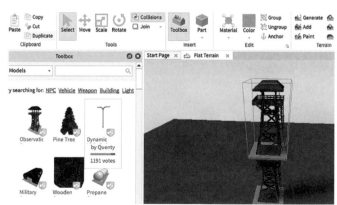

CLIPBOARD: The Clipboard section is made up of a few different general tools. They're usually found on Paint and Word processing programs on the computer.

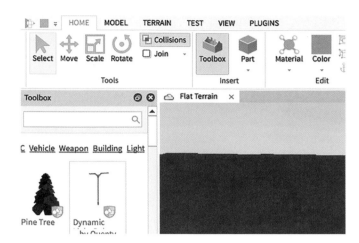

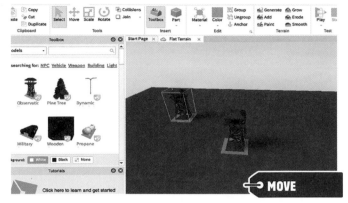

MASTER BUILDER ROBLOX

TOOLS: With help from the tools section, you can modify items that you choose based on their location and angle. You can move them, turn them, make them larger and more with these tools. They're located to the right of the Clipboard section on the HOME tab.

ACTION	DESCRIPTION
SELECT	Use this to click on an item and move it around the screen to where you'd like it to go while also highlighting it.
MOVE	The move command allows you to click on items that are not highlighted and move them to various places on the terrain.
SCALE	Change the size of the shape making it larger or smaller, depending on what your goal is in the game.
ROTATE	Rotate the object around to face a different direction using the provided balls with this tool. Just be sure to swivel yourself as well using your mouse, to keep a good view while rotating objects.
COLLISIONS	You can choose whether or not items should overlap each other with this tool. It detects when they do and fixes it for you.
JOIN	This tool joins two items together within a game. Use it to decide what items to join, to have them automatically join when placed together, or to never join. You can even set objects to only join to building terrain, and nothing else.

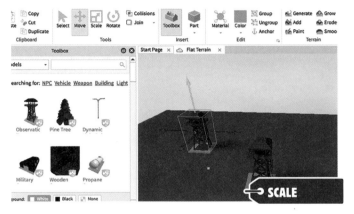

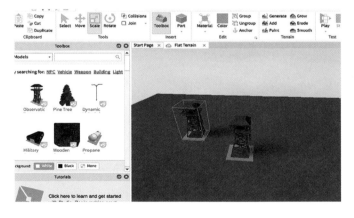

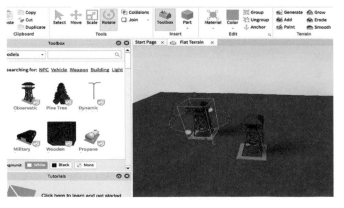

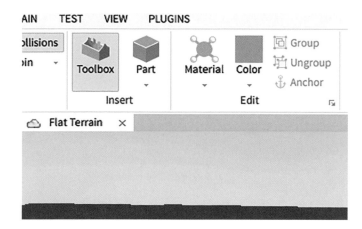

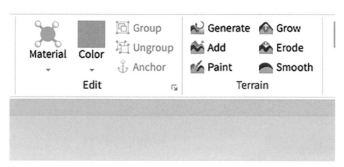

Choose between a block, sphere, wedge or cylinder part to add to the builder to make a unique creation. This option is also available in the HOME tab.

INSERT: This area is where you'll find ways to create your own part to be modeled into the game. You have the option to show the toolbox on the left of the screen, or remove it entirely. Getting rid of it will give you more screen space to make your own creations.

EDIT: The Edit function allows you to change the look and feel of parts you've added into the game already. Once you choose the shape of the part, it should be shown on the screen. However, this is not how you want it to look in the game, which means you have to change it using the functions described below.

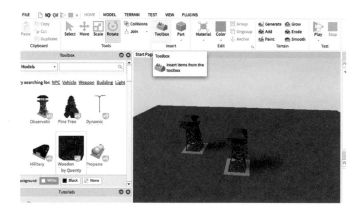

Click on the Toolbox button to shrink it down and select it again to keep it open on the left. Keeping the box open gives you easy access to the items inside if you'll be frequently adding objects while creating your world. If you're not using it while building the terrain, then you can remove the Toolbox from the side of the work space with another click.

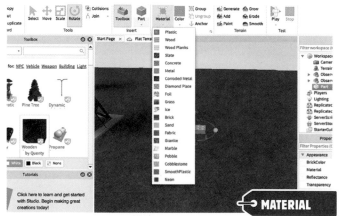

ACTION	DESCRIPTION
MATERIAL	The material can be changed to provide a different look and feel. There are many to choose from such as wood, concrete, ice, slate, fabric, grass, sand and so on. Choosing the one that closely relates to the item you're trying to build will give it the right look.
COLOR	The color can be chosen to closely design the item that you're building. It's important to select a color that matches your object closely. You can choose from the honeycomb of colors provided in the drop down box for just the right one.

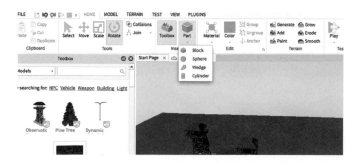

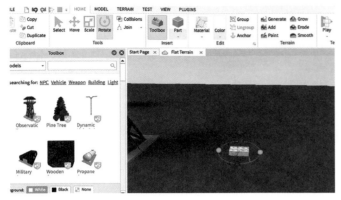

ACTION — DESCRIPTION

ACTION	DESCRIPTION
GROUP	This creates a group of items and moves them together, almost as a single object would be moved. The button can create a cluster effect within the game. Which is helpful when dealing with many objects.
UNGROUP	Use this to ungroup the items within the group already. In order for this function to work, the items have to originally be grouped together.
ANCHOR	This determines if the parts should remain in one place during game play or be able to move around. Those anchored will not move at all helping you to create a more stable world.

TERRAIN: The terrain tools allow you to change the overall look and feel of the ground and land in the game. With the use of this tool, you can make the area look however you'd like.

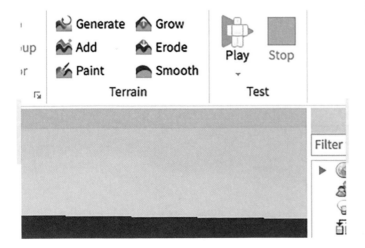

ACTION	DESCRIPTION
GENERATE	Generate another piece of land on top of what you already have. Choose the size and type of biome you'd like the new terrain to have, such as a body of water or swamp. This will then be added to the existing world's terrain.
ADD	Easily add any type of material onto the land by painting it on. Choose the type of material you'd like to put in the area, such as water, marble, sand and then use the brush to place it wherever you'd like. This option lets you go up with the material — such as building a wall.
PAINT	Paint works in the same way as ADD, the only difference is that it only works on the ground. So you can create a walkway, path, body of water, marble patio and so on.
GROW	Create hills, tall water falls, statues and more with the Grow function. You just have to click on the material that you want to use and then you can easily move the specified area up to create the item.
ERODE	Erode works in the opposite way compared to Grow. You can create tunnels and underground passages, or just large craters in the terrain in the world. Simply place the mouse over where you want to erode and start removing land.
SMOOTH	Use the Smooth function to create smoother edges on some of the jagged areas throughout the terrain. This could be anything from rocks to tunnels, to hills you've created. Glide the mouse over the area you want to smooth down.

With each of these functions, you'll be able to adjust the size, shape and strength of the actions you're trying to perform. This gives you more precise control over your creations.

The shape will allow you to create different looking mountains, make different bodies of water and so on.

Control the size of the command that you're performing through the use of the sliding scale that makes the area bigger or smaller. This tool works well if you want to scale to size the material that you're using on the land.

The strength is how much you want to put into the command. If you're creating a shallow puddle, you want less strength as compared to building a large lake. You want to have less strength for a small hill as compared to a large mountain.

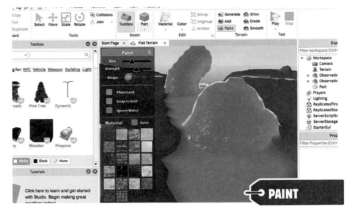

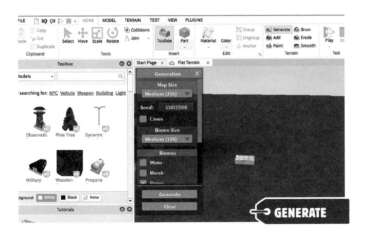

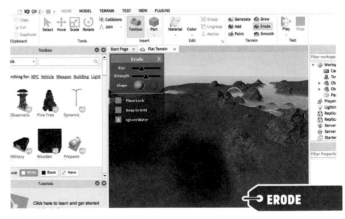

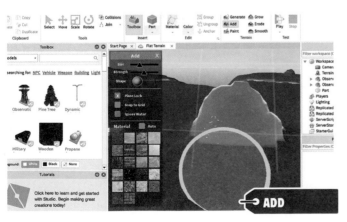

TEST: Testing is just as it says. You get to test out the creative world that you've just made!

This is a great way to make sure you know it works before publishing it or to find other aspects that need to be changed before you put it out to the general public.

Click on PLAY — Choose Play, Play Here or Run

ACTION	DESCRIPTION
PLAY	Use this button to go around and make sure that everything is working as it should. It will put your player in the game, without having to open up the Roblox Player to do so. This is great when you're still working on the game and do not want to get back in the studio each time you need to fix something.
PLAY HERE	Play Here allows you to play right in the Roblox Studio where you're currently viewing the world. This does not put you at the starting point, which is what general Play will do if you were to click that.

This is ideal if you're going to be testing out a specific item in this location and would like to start and stop in this area. |

ACTION	DESCRIPTION
RUN	Run the game without being a player in the world through this option. You can check everything out by just floating above it to see what it will look like inside the actual world.
STOP	In order to stop the game play, you have to click on the red square labeled STOP at the top. You then are brought back to the editor area where you can continue to create the items in the world.

Alternatively, you could just click the play button, without bringing down the menu using the small arrow. This will put you right into game play without having to choose a specific way to play the game.

There are a lot of functions and tabs that can be used inside these worlds. Each command has a different action, allowing you to completely customize your world as a whole. You do not have to worry about not being able to have enough tools to do what you want.

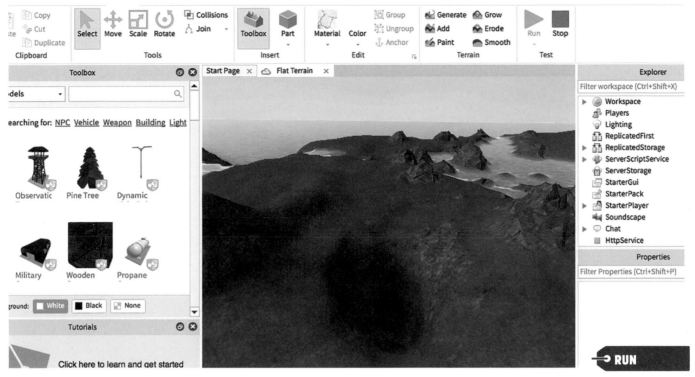

In addition to these quick edit and create tools within the Roblox Studio, Lua provides you with a wide array of other commands, once you learn the programming language. With help from the programming language, you can create a lot of your own settings, items and designs without having to use what's provided to you through the Studio and the creations that other people have made in the toolbox.

Learn more about the tabs at the top that help you create your world in the next chapters, while also exploring a bit more about Lua, the programming language that has been helping kids like you design worlds of their own.

ROBLOX STUDIO TABS: MODEL

The second out of six tabs that can be found at the top of the Roblox Studio Editor is the MODEL tab. This tool gives you the ability to adjust and manipulate all the different objects throughout your world.

The tools in this tab are essential to adjusting the look and feel of your world. Without them you won't be able to customize your creations much.

When using these tabs, it is important to note that some of them have mini functions within a function. There is a small arrow pointing down that you can click on for additional functions.

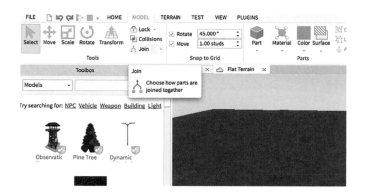

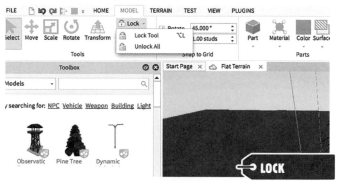

MODEL:
You've already gone through and modified the terrain of your world, customizing the look of the land, now it's time to explore the MODEL tab.

Click on the MODEL tab right next to the HOME tab at the top of the editor. This opens up a lengthy list of options for you to make use of.

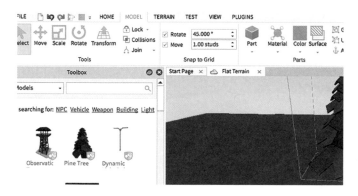

TOOLS:
Many of the same functions that were found on the HOME tab carry over into the MODEL tab. If you're unsure of what these areas can do, go back to the previous chapter. They are SELECT, MOVE, SCALE, ROTATE, COLLISIONS and JOIN.

There are however, a few new ones in this TOOLS section that you can use in the MODEL tab while creating your world.

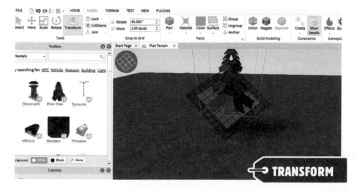

ACTION	DESCRIPTION
TRANSFORM	Designed to supplement the other tools — MOVE, SCALE and ROTATE, the tool allows you to do all 3 of these moves with just one click of the tool. You can move, position and resize the object.
LOCK	The lock tool provides the user with a way to lock the parts that they've created so that they cannot be manipulated by the editor tools. There are two options with this tool — Lock Tool and Unlock All. When the items on the editor are unlocked (shown with an unlocked lock) then the items can be manipulated. If they're locked (locked lock) then you cannot remove them.

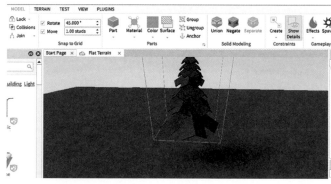

SNAP TO GRID:
An option provided at the top tool bar. This function allows you to resize blocks and other objects that you put into the world. To resize the objects you adjust their numbers and create sizes based off of your world itself. This results in more perfect creations that are sized exactly the way you want them to be. This tool is much more exact than the scale tool, making it easy to precisely adjust different objects.

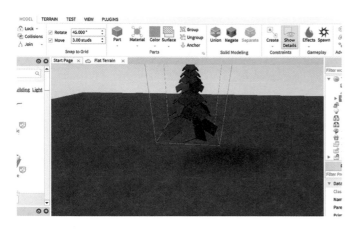

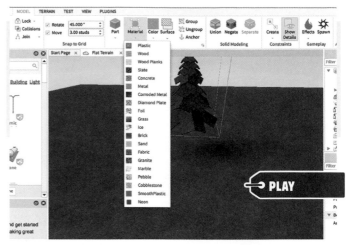

PARTS: Creating objects has never been easier with the use of the PARTS section. Not only can you create just about anything, these tools make it easy to smooth out objects, change their color or just create new things from scratch to put into your world.

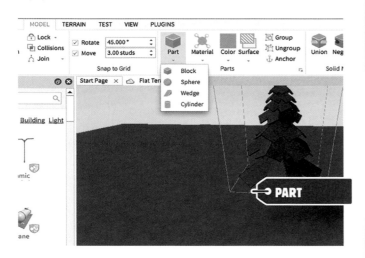

ACTION	DESCRIPTION
PART	This option provides four different parts that you can place into game play and create into anything you want. Choose from BLOCK, SPHERE, WEDGE or CYLINDER. Each one will show up on the terrain, allowing you to manipulate it with the tools.
MATERIAL	There are 20 different materials you can choose from on the list. This allows you to make the PART that you chose into something. You can choose to have it be a block of wood, or a stone. You can choose a granite piece to make into a countertop and so on.
COLOR	The color wheel that is presented allows you to change the color of the PART that you have. Once you choose the PART and the MATERIAL, you can then color it. Granite or marble will still have that marble looking appearance, as will wood and other materials, but it will be in the color of your choice.
SURFACE	Choose the surface of the PART that you have. You can go with a grainy surface, ideal for sand or dirt or a smooth one if you're making a countertop or other smooth item. There are 9 different surfaces you can choose from to change the overall shape and feel of the PART.
GROUP/ UNGROUP	Group and Ungroup were both discussed in the previous chapter. They allow you to create a cluster of items within the game, or ungroup them to remove the cluster.
ANCHOR	Another Tool described in the previous chapter. The Anchor function provides a way for you to create stand-alone products in one place during game play or allow them to be moveable actionable pieces in the game.

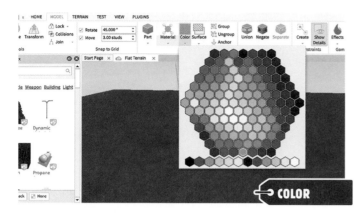

COLOR

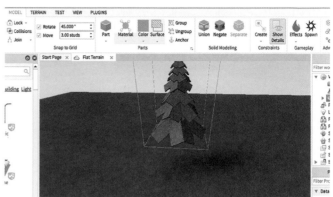

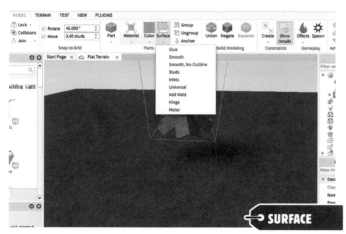

SURFACE

Here, I've used the PART, MATERIAL, COLOR and SURFACE tools to create a brick wall in my world. I chose a BLOCK and then resized it. I chose to go with a BRICK material and then changed the color to be RED. I also made it into a smooth surface.

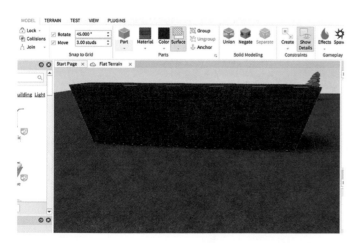

SOLID MODELING: All of the options provided in the SOLID MODELING section allow you to create very complex shapes from very simple shapes. You can create just about any shape you can imagine with help from these tools.

Additionally, if you're using several parts to make up an object, using SOLID MODELING for them instead allows the game to run much faster and smoother than having to use all the separate parts to make up the object.

ACTION	DESCRIPTION
UNION	To use the UNION tool select two objects next to one another and select union to connect them. The same can be done with all of the parts of the item. This should only be done on basic parts that you have.
NEGATE	Negate is a cool feature that makes creating unions simple, and allows you to make entirely new objects. Select two objects and put them together in a way that you want. Now use the NEGATE tool on both of them and all the overlapping parts will disappear, leaving you with a clean, unique shape.
SEPARATE	Undo the union that you created, if you do not like it by using the SEPARATE feature. This allows you to erase the union and start over with something new.

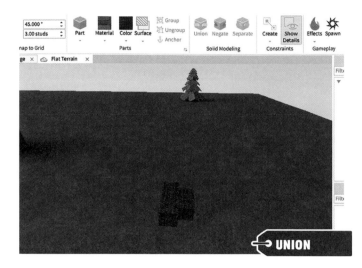

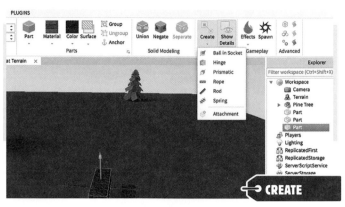

UNION

CREATE

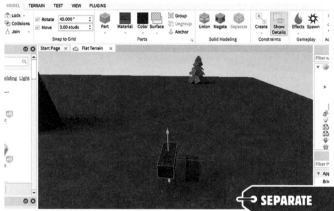

SEPARATE

ACTION	DESCRIPTION
CREATE	Create provides 7 options for you to choose from. You can add a single thread like item to the items that you're building by using this function. If you want to create a rope for hanging clothes or tightrope walking, you would use this function. Additionally, you could create a spring, rod, hinge or other detailed part to add unique features to your current construction.
SHOW DETAILS	This function allows the player to see the details of where the object was created and placed on the items. This can give you an idea of what you can move, resize or add to the section. With this function off, you cannot see where the object was placed and it looks like a normal part of the game. In

CONSTRAINTS: When you want to tie something down, or provide a spring-like appearance to the items that you're creating, then you'd use this function. It provides you with a way to contain the items that you've already made in the game through the use of 7 different items. It can complete the look or provide further actionable objects within the game.

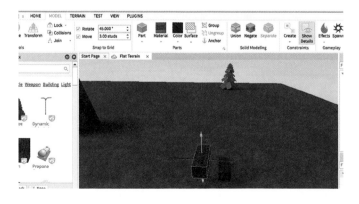

SHOW DETAILS

the picture above I created a rope that brought my two bricks together. This can be done with any of the CREATE objects in the option field and then connected by clicking on one object and then dragging the mouse cursor over to the other.

GAMEPLAY:
During game play, you'll likely want a few features that stand out to your world users. This can be done through the use of effects. There are 8 different special effects in all, giving you plenty of options to choose from when modifying different objects. Additionally, during game play, a player may choose to enter into the game and this is where you will adjust their spawn location into your world.

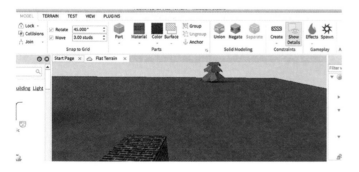

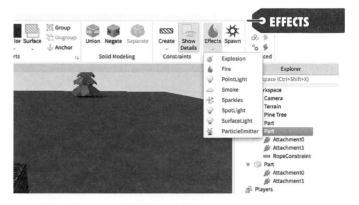

ACTION	DESCRIPTION
EFFECTS	The effects section allows you to change the atmosphere in the world with special enhancements. You can add actions and animations to your creations with this tool. If you wanted to create a large explosion in the world, this can be done with this function. Additionally, creating a fireplace with fire inside it can also be added. Lighting is another one. You have 8 different options to choose from.
SPAWN	The SPAWN option is is a tool that determines where players start off in your world. When they begin the game, or each time they die, they will start off at their assigned spawn location.

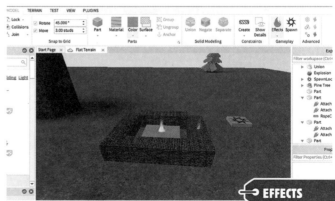

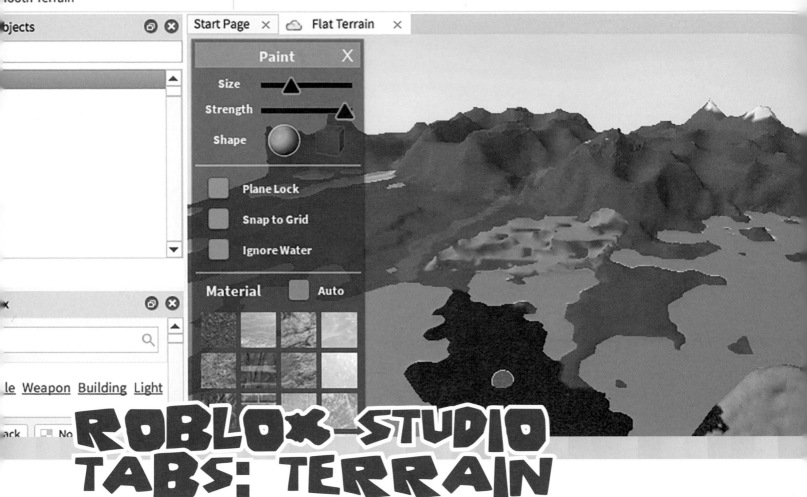

ROBLOX STUDIO TABS: TERRAIN

The editor is designed with many tabs that allow you to change and manipulate the items, terrain and specific functions around you in the world. Here we're going to focus specifically on the TERRAIN tab. This tool makes it easy to change the terrain or land around you.

The tool is ideal for helping the shape of your world fit with its overall theme. You can add hills, holes or smooth out the land in front of you.

Through the useful tools provided in this section, you can dramatically change the look and feel of your world to anything that you would like.

Ready to change the entire foundation that you're building on? Let's get started!

GENERATE: This tool lets you change the entire outside appearance of your land. Not only can you click the specific biomes that you want, but you can also choose how large you want the land and biome to be. For example, if you want a specific biome or environment surrounded by flat terrain on one or more of the sides, you can choose a large map and position a small biome somewhere in it.

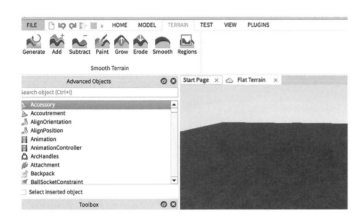

When choosing the biome, you can check and uncheck all of the items you want or don't want your land to be. Once you do this, clicking on GENERATE will spawn your new environment into life. A status bar will pop up and load as the world changes to include or remove the items you've checked off.

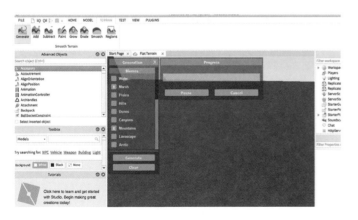

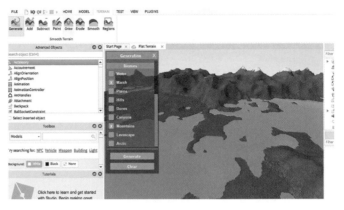

I made my land into a marshy wetland with mountains off in the distance. I took away the flat plains in the immediate area, while making the map bigger so that there was more flat land in the distance to add additional buildings and creations.

You can play around with this feature to learn exactly what your options are and what you can do. The main thing is making sure to get the scenery right to match the theme of your world nicely.

ADD: This tool makes it easy to add specific items to an existing world. Once the box pops up there are many options to choose from that allow you to personalize your world however you'd like.

With the click of a button you can add in materials to the area such as sand, gravel, grass, concrete, brick and others. You can click on the IGNORE WATER feature if you'd like to make sure that these items do not go over the water. If you decide that you want to create a bridge or floating walkway or something, it's quick and easy to uncheck that feature and start building right on top of the water.

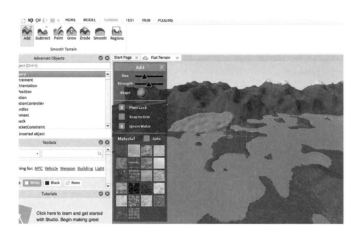

I accented my world with a nice sandy beach at the edge of the water down below one of my mountains. You can add whatever you'd like, and it's fun to get really creative with it. You can also change the size and shape of the tool allowing you to place a variety of sizes down. Just by moving the arrows up or down on the sliding scales, you can change the size and strength of the materials being placed. Choose either a sphere or cube to put down the right shape for your purposes.

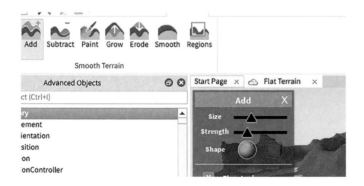

SUBTRACT: Subtract works almost the same way that an eraser would. It will gradually take away materials starting with a small amount and increasing with each pass you make. To fully remove materials quickly, you'll have to turn the eraser strength up higher before using the tool.

If you want to add lumps or to shave some of the material down to give it a different look, you can use this feature for that, as well. I used the feature to create dunes across the sand and give them a bumpier appearance.

Subtract is a simple tool to use and it doesn't need much clarification. You just choose the size, shape and strength of the eraser and then click and go over the areas of materials you'd like to remove from the world.

PAINT: Roblox also gives you a pretty cool tool that actually lets you change the material of objects and terrain, and it's called PAINT.

Don't like how one material looks or want to give it a facelift? Then you'd use the PAINT function to get the job done. It can be found in TERRAIN.

You can choose the size, strength and shape of your paint brush and get to work. You can choose from 22 different types of paint materials. Once you've made your choice, you can lock specific planes, or water surfaces, to keep the painted material only where you want it to be. That makes it easy to quickly cover large areas of your terrain and alter it just the way you want it to be.

PAINT was a great tool for creating lava in the water, as well as creating a stone walkway.

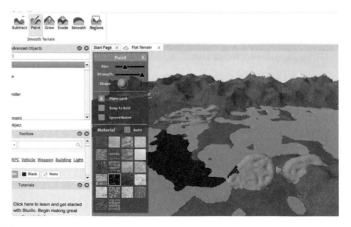

GROW: The GROW feature gives you a tool to easily adjust the size of water, land and other features of your terrain quickly. You just choose an area and material that you'd like to grow, as well as the size, shape and strength and then place your mouse over it to start the transformation. Hold down on the mouse button to adjust the size of the material right in front of your eyes.

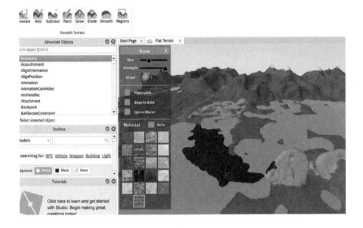

This can help you make many things such as hills, mountains, blocks of land, raised pathways and even large tsunamis or fountains. You can be as creative as you'd like with the use of the GROW tool.

You can change and shape anything in the world that you can think of with the grow tool and with enough practice you'll be able to make some cool creations with it.

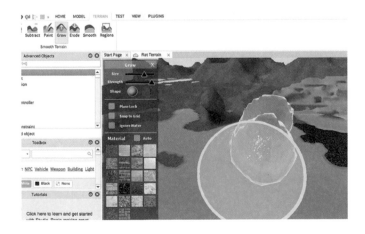

ERODE: ERODE works in the same way that GROW does. You just dig down instead of building up with this feature, which makes it useful for a number of things. If you want to add a ditch, stream or an underground cave type of area, then this tool works wonderfully.

You can use the ERODE function both on land and in water. It doesn't matter where you choose to use it. You can make the holes as large or small as you'd like them to be. Let your creativity roam free and create cool passageways and unique areas in your world. You can impress your visitors, or you can trap them!

There are many ways to make the ERODE function useful when it comes to creating your own world or game and being as creative as possible with it.

SMOOTH: The SMOOTH tool, located up at the top, is good for smoothing out land and other surfaces. It blends different sections of the terrain together. If you want to blend the sand into the grass and then the water, you'd just run the smooth tool along the edges using your mouse.

If you want to create an underground passage but don't want to deal with the jagged edges around you and want to make it look nice, then you can go into the tunnel and smooth your way through those areas.

The SMOOTH tool does not erase or even completely flatten down areas, but it does provide a way for you to make areas on the map smoother and blended in with the other surroundings. This makes it easier to create that finished look that you'd want whether you're creating a unique world, a beach, a ski resort or anything else, this tool can come in handy.

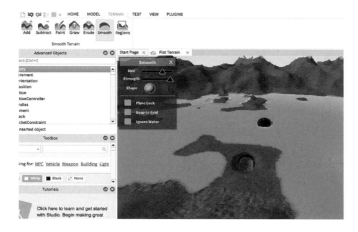

REGIONS: This option has a few different tools that you can utilize depending on what it is that you want to do. The tools work well for splitting up different parts of the world, copy and pasting them to new locations or other neat tricks to shape your world in additional ways.

ACTION	DESCRIPTION
SELECT	This allows you to select a region anywhere on your world. You can then choose one of the other options to manipulate it any way you'd like.
MOVE	Move the desired selected region to another area on the map. Once there you can fine-tune its location further by moving it up or over. You can move all types of terrain, including water.
RESIZE	You can make an area bigger or smaller depending on your preference with this tool. If you just moved a piece of the water and want to make a larger pond area than what you have, the resize tool will make quick work of the task.
ROTATE	Rotate a single terrain section with this tool. This can make it stand up like a wall, or even turn to face a different direction.
COPY	Copy the same section of terrain to a new area, while keeping the existing piece in the original location.
PASTE	Put down a copied section of terrain into a new location.
DELETE	Delete the selected region of your choosing. Use this tool to remove copies you no longer want, or to create completely blank areas ready for future edits.
FILL	Fill an area of terrain with a specific material. This provides you with a way to create an island, place different platforms around the area or anything else that you can think of.

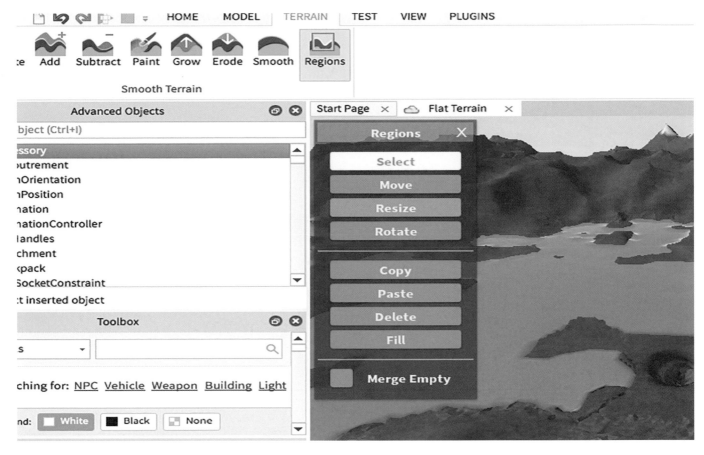

Merge Empty is a box that can be left checked or unchecked. When the box is checked, this will fill all the cells around the selected area when it comes to filling in the selection. However, if you have it checked then it is only going to fill in the cells that have been selected.

When designing a different look and feel to the terrain in your world, you have to make sure that it works with the world or game that you're creating. You want something that's going to go with the main idea or 'theme' and that will actually add to it, instead of taking away from your desired appearance.

Most of the time the terrain of your game is going to make a huge difference when it comes to game play and how other players will enjoy the look and feel of a game. Make sure you do everything possible to create a convincing environment, which means editing the terrain dramatically.

When you go to use all the different terrain tools, take your time to get to know them and all they can do. You might be surprised at how many tools are really available to you. You shouldn't have to worry about not being able to change the way one thing looks or creating the right amount of marsh, mountains, plains, water and other areas with the use of the many tools provided.

As always, have fun and check out the next chapter to learn even more about what the Roblox Editor can do for you.

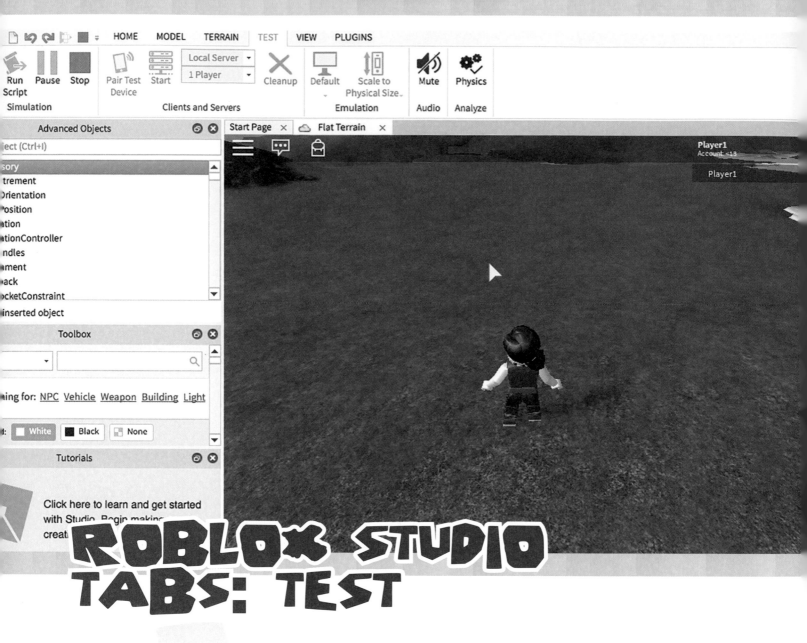

ROBLOX STUDIO TABS: TEST

When it comes to testing out the world that you've just created, there is a whole tab to help you get the job done. Not only should you try your game to make sure it's fun before you publish it, but you should also thoroughly test it to be sure it's running properly.

The TEST tab is designed specifically for testing purposes and will help you find any issues with the game play and see how your scripts are functioning.

Th test tool is an excellent way to find out how well your world works, and you won't know until you try!

Test out the game that you created today and see how well it works when you're the player in the middle of it all!

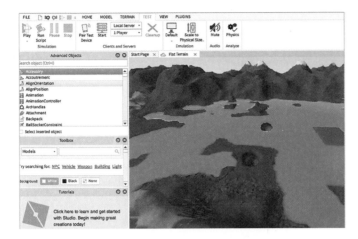

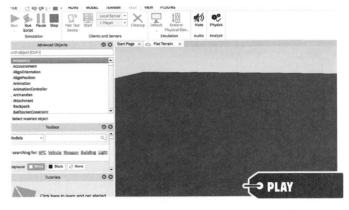

The test tab has a few options to choose from when you open it up. These options are all related to actually testing the game out in real-time game play. Depending on the terrain, objects and script that you've used throughout the game, you need to make sure it works.

This can all be done in the testing tab with the tools explained below.

SIMULATION: Simulation allows you to perform tasks associated with playing the actual game. This is where you'd start, stop and continue the game play. You can also check out how scripts run in the game during play with the option here.

ACTION	DESCRIPTION
PLAY	Play has a few options that open up underneath it when you click it — Play, Play Here, Run. All of these options allow you to customize how you run the game during the test mode. **Play** — You are spawned into the place you've put your spawning pad. **Play Here** — Drops you where you're currently positioned so you can check out the immediate items in that area. **Run** — This allows you to run the world without having any characters in it. This can be useful when trying to see how the world will look to other players that enter, without having characters in the way.

ACTION	DESCRIPTION
RUN SCRIPT	In order to make the game play how you'd like it to, especially if it is a more involved type of game, you're going to have to run a script in order to make it do so. This can be done using the Run Script feature. You just have to upload the script from your computer to place it in the game.
PAUSE	You can pause the game play at any time by hitting the pause button at the top. This will keep the game live, but it will pause everything temporarily. You just have to press run again to start everything up once again.
STOP	Stop works to stop the game play. If you want to go back to editing the game or need to fix something in the game, then you'd press stop and go to another one of the tabs at the top to do so.

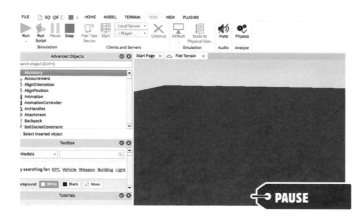

CLIENTS AND SERVERS:
In order to get a real feel for how the entire game is going to turn out, it's important to test it in a real server/client environment. That's when you'll see the game the way that other people will view it. So load up a local client and make sure your game will connect to it properly and that everything is going to run the way that it should.

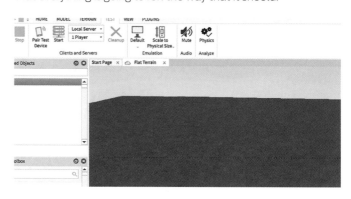

ACTION	DESCRIPTION
PAIR TEST DEVICE	If you play using the iOS app, you can use this feature to pair your world with an iOS device. This provides you with a way to check the iOS settings and ensure that they run smoothly on.this app.
START	This starts the simulation of the server and players within the game. You will be brought to another window that pops open which is the server.
SERVER/ PLAYERS	You can choose to use the local server, or a specially made one if you add it to the list. If you want to test more than one player, you can choose the number of players you want from the drop-down menu.
CLEANUP	This closes all of the testing within the server and brings you back to the original Roblox Studio Editor.

PAIR TEST

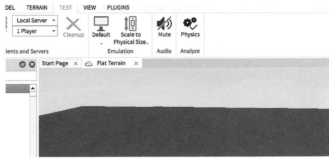

ACTION — DESCRIPTION

DEFAULT

You choose which device you'd like to see the game on. Each choice provides a different type of device with a different size. It then will change the size and shape of the game to fit the device that is chosen.

SCALE TO PHYSICAL SIZE

You can choose how large the resolution is, as well as scaling the picture to the physical size of the screen. This can be tricky to mess with, depending on how you'd want the layout to look on other devices. The calibration of scaling can be done to ensure that the viewing area works properly on different devices.

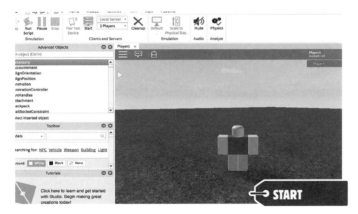

START

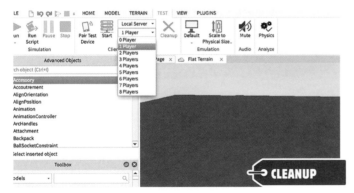

CLEANUP

EMULATION: Find out how your game performs across different devices, whether you're using a smartphone of any type, a different computer, a tablet and so on. You can make sure that the game functions work the same way they would on the computer.

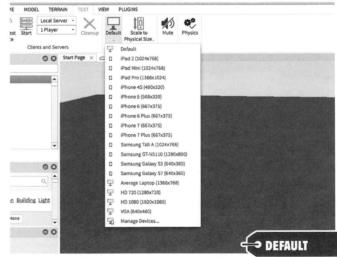

DEFAULT

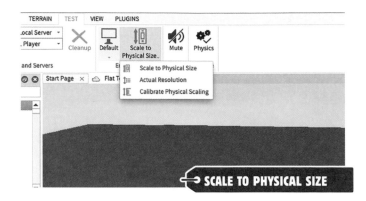

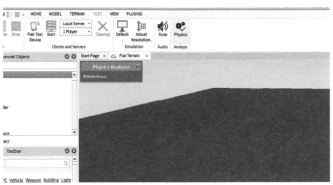

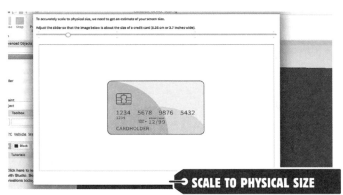

ANALYZE:

ANALYZE: This section is the Physics Analyzer. This is a very useful tool. When the game is being played, you can go through and continue to play it without worrying about what is wrong. The analyzer is going to be the one that picks up on things not working right throughout the entire game.

This means, this can do the work for you, especially if you're new to creating your own world. You want to make sure to read what the analyzer has found and fix any problems that may pop up in the editor.

This can be a useful tool when it comes to finding and solving problems throughout the game that might cause it to not function properly.

This is a short tab section that allows you to go through your game to make sure it is all working properly. Without the use of this tab, a lot of game makers would have to go through their games once they're live and try to figure out the problems. This can cause a lot of trouble with the back and forth that they'd have to do.

Once you're finished with your world, always go to this tab and use it to your advantage. It's important to test the world before it goes public, that way the game is uninterrupted by bugs or small fixes that have to be made.

In the next section we'll cover the VIEW tab, where you can learn even more about the game and what you can do to make your own come to life.

AUDIO:

AUDIO: The AUDIO section of the bar allows you to toggle the sounds. This provides you with the ability to turn game sounds on and off in the editor, allowing you to hear what the game will really sound like.

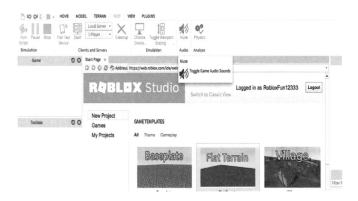

A quick press of this button switches the sound on or off. This is a personal choice and does not change anything in the game that you're making.

ROBLOX STUDIO TABS: VIEW

The VIEW tabs give game creators the tools they need to monitor their worlds, make sure scripts are running properly and to see things like error messages. They're advanced problem-solving utilities and special features that give you more power when trying to run or improve a Roblox world. It also allows you to toggle between views both on your editor and during game play.

When you know how to utilize the VIEW tab properly, you can solve world problems and create more effectively.

This is mostly for testing and monitoring scripts within a world, and doesn't focus on actual gameplay itself. Get your coding pants on, and find out all that comes with this diagnostics toolpack.

Here's an overview of each of the tools and what they're designed to do.

SHOW: Use this section to look at details about objects that actually show on your screen when the game is running.

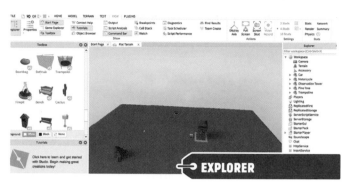

EXPLORER

ACTION	DESCRIPTION
EXPLORER	This feature provides the user with a list of the different items, services and instances that are in the game. You can then modify them by using the menu on the right.
PROPERTIES	This option allows you to see all of the properties of the selected object in the game.
START PAGE	This brings up the original page where you selected the terrain of your choice in a new, smaller window. Toggle between the tabs at the top to choose which page you want to be on.
GAME EXPLORER	Read the game data in the box that pops up on the left-hand side. This can only be done once the game is published on a public server and is being used by other players.
TOOL BOX	This button brings up or lowers the object tool box that you can pull items from to put into your game. If you're done adding objects, you won't make use of the Tool Box.
CONTEXT HELP	If you want more information on a currently selected item and an explanation of what it does, this area will bring up the Wiki page from Roblox that explains it for you.

PROPERTIES

START PAGE

GAME EXPLORER

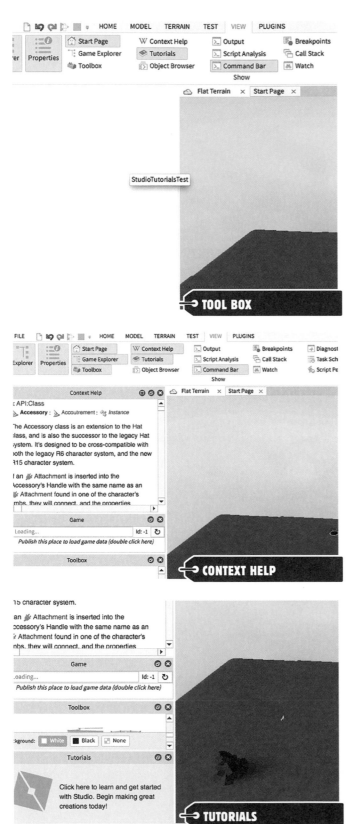

ACTION / DESCRIPTION

ACTION	DESCRIPTION
TUTORIALS	This is where you can find many Roblox tutorials that the makers have developed to help you during the build mode portion of the game. If you ever get stuck in a spot, go here for a quick lesson.
OBJECT BROWSER	This displays information on every object, class and other item within the game. You can do a search for a specific item to find what you're looking to learn more about.
OUTPUT	This section displays errors and problem codes from the different scripts in your game. You'll see them at the bottom of the screen.
SCRIPT ANALYSIS	This shows script warnings, errors and problems right when you put the scripts in the game without having to run the game to find them.
COMMAND BAR	The command bar is where you can place Lua codes to modify your world in different ways. These are different than the standard scripts.
BREAKPOINTS	This section allows you to establish breakpoints and monitor them to isolate Lua errors more accurately.

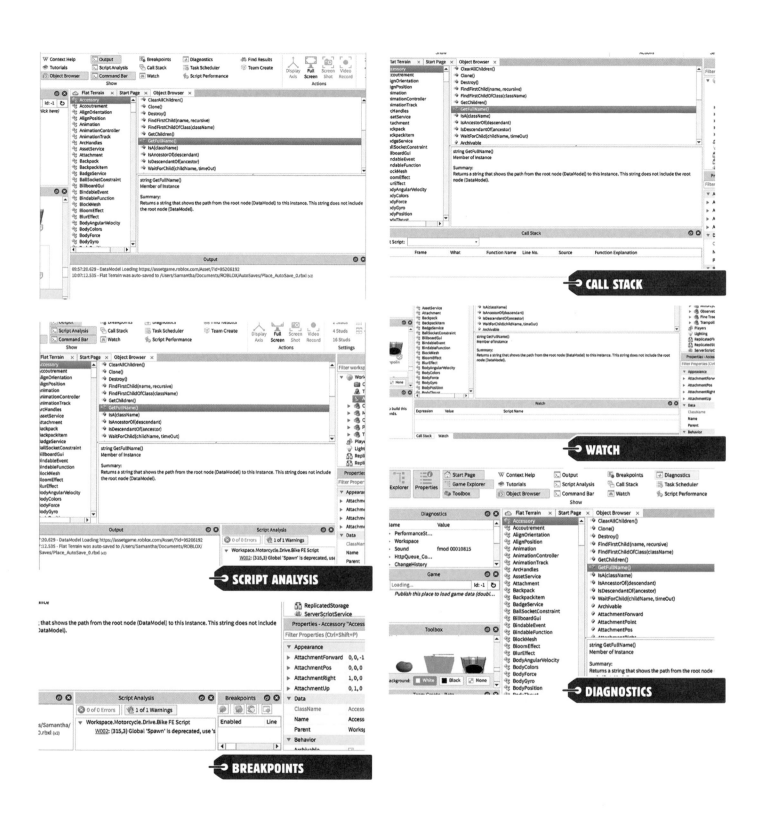

SCRIPT ANALYSIS

BREAKPOINTS

CALL STACK

WATCH

DIAGNOSTICS

ACTION	DESCRIPTION
CALL STACK	When you pause the game, this shows you where the code in the game is currently. This is a powerful tool for finding and fixing errors.
WATCH	Use this to easily see all the variables and conditions you have set to watch.
DIAGNOSTICS	Find out the status of your game while it is running with this box that provides feedback.
TASK SCHEDULER	See feedback on any looping services that you have running in your game during game play.
SCRIPT PERFORMANCE	Shows CPU usage in relation to your game's scripts. Use it to pinpoint resource hogging features that could be slowing down your game.
FIND RESULTS	When you search using CTRL+SHIFT+F, this is where your results for that search will be displayed.
TEAM CREATE	If you want to build and edit a world with friends, this is where you'd go to do so. You can all work in the team mode to provide the right game for many others to play.

SCRIPT PERFORMANCE

TEAM CREATE

TASK SCHEDULER

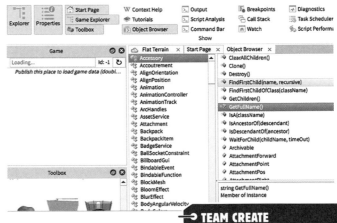

TEAM CREATE

ACTION: Actions are special tools you can use while running the game. With everything from recording video to capturing screen shots, you can make sure to get the most out of the world you create when you use these functions.

ACTION	DESCRIPTION
DISPLAY AXIS	Display an axis at the bottom of the screen of the world that you've created. This provides you with the dimensions of the entire world.
FULL SCREEN	Toggle the screen on full or partial screen views using this option.
SCREEN SHOT	Take a screen shot of the game where you're currently in it. If you move around, you can get different screen shots of different views.
VIDEO RECORD	When this option is chosen it provides a red box around the area that it is recording for you. Once done, clicking the option again will stop the recording and save the video for later use.

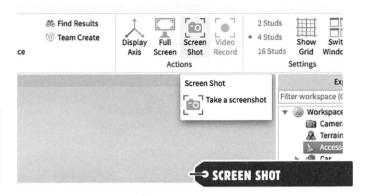

SCREEN SHOT

SETTINGS: Adjust the views of the game using these settings. Some change the way the game is played, others alter how it is viewed and still some change how it is built, so they're all pretty important depending on what you are trying to accomplish.

2, 4, 16 STUDS

ACTION	DESCRIPTION
2, 4, 16 STUDS	This option allows you to change the view of the studs. If the SHOW GRIDS option is on, you can set the view to show 2, 4 or 16 studs at a time.
SHOW GRIDS	This is an X Y axis grid that is shown on the screen to allow you to better adjust the layout of the world.
SWITCH WINDOWS	If you have multiple tabs or windows open in the editor that you're working on, this allows you to change back and forth between them.

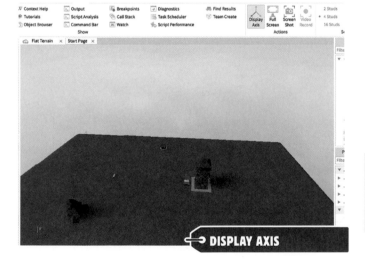

DISPLAY AXIS

2, 4, 16 STUDS

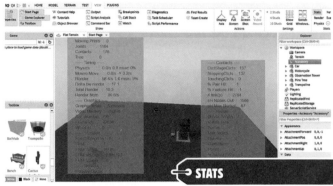

STATS

2, 4, 16 STUDS

ACTION	DESCRIPTION
STATS	This is where you'd find general diagnostics information regarding the game and game play.
RENDER	This shows the diagnostics information on a display for the game.
PHYSICS	Keep an eye on all physics simulations running in your world here.
NETWORK	Learn more about the game's network and how it is running.
SUMMARY	This is where the high level, advanced information can be found.
CUSTOM	This is where you can create a customized statistics spreadsheet of the game diagnostics.
CLEAR (RED CIRCLE WITH -)	Remove all of the stats that you pulled up on the screen, off the screen when this button is clicked.

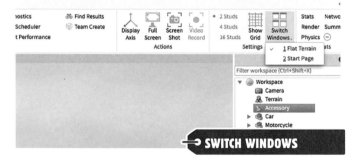

SWITCH WINDOWS

STATS: This is where you're going to find all of the diagnostics information for the game and game play. You'll get information about the actual world itself, and also how it's running for other players as they are experiencing the world. It's very important when you actually start making your new world available to the public.

RENDER

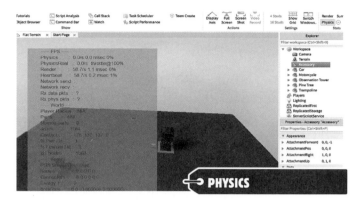

PHYSICS

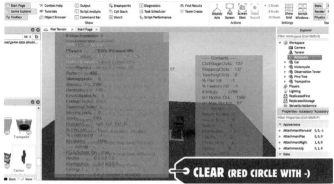

CLEAR (RED CIRCLE WITH -)

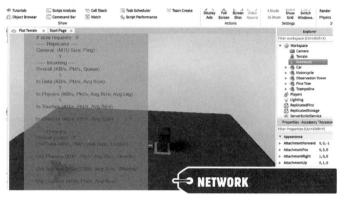

NETWORK

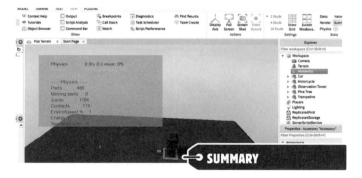

SUMMARY

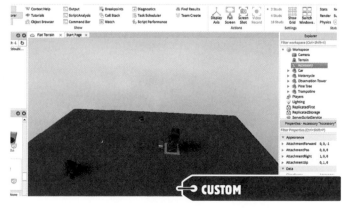

CUSTOM

Views give you everything that you need to view, run and test different aspects of your game world. That's why it's so important to learn how to use the tools if you plan on making a world of your own. Take the time to familiarize yourself with each of the differnet tools and what they can do for you.

Understanding how to do a diagnostics test will help you troubleshoot any problems that you run into while creating a new world. Whether you are working with friends, or creating on your own, you'll find a use for many of the tools in the VIEWS tab.

No matter what type of world you decide to create, make sure you have fun doing it!

This is Roblox your way, all the time. You can be as creative as you'd like and create new exciting worlds to share with other people. The diagnostic tools discussed above should help you accomplish that goal, but it's important to remember that it's really about having fun. So play around, add features that you want, and try to make worlds you and your friends can be excited about.

Check out the next chapter that talks about the last tab in the editor mode - PLUGINS. You can learn more about the additional content, or plugins that you can add to the game and make the most of them!

ROBLOX STUDIO TABS: PLUGINS

Plugins are additional content that you can add to your game. Whether you want to make something happen within the game, change the overall look and feel, create a different game base or anything else, these plugins can provide you with a way to do so.

You can go to the Roblox published folder on the website. This is the library, next to the My Creations tab that allows you to search for specific plugins that others have made. You can also just make your scripts through Lua and then save them to your My Creations folder. This provides you with a way to use your own plugins.

When making a plugin, you can publish it to the library folder for other developers to use within their games. It is ultimately your choice on what you do and how you use the plugins that you create. You can also use another developer's plugin you download from the website in one of your games to save time.

The plugins can be added through this tab in the editor. You just have to remember where you save the plugins to, since you'll have to later find the folder that allows you to upload them to the game.

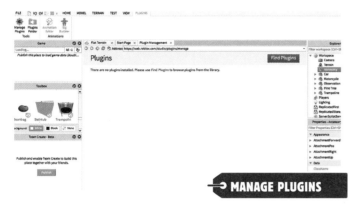

MANAGE PLUGINS

TOOLS: These are the tools you're going to use to upload, manage and use the plugins within the world or game that you're making. You need to be able to use these if you want to add extras into the game.

ACTIONS	DESCRIPTION
MANAGE PLUGINS	You can manage all of the plugins that you add to the game through this editor. You just have to pull up the plugins and then open them. This way, you can fix, edit or remove them from the game.
PLUGINS FOLDER	The plugins folder is where you're going to find all of the plugins that you've made and saved or that you've downloaded from the library on the website. Once clicked, these plugins will then be added to your game.

Keep in mind, once you add the plugins to the game, you will want to go back and run a diagnostics test, as well as testing the game play again. This is to ensure that the plugins you added to the game are working to the best of their ability and that there are no issues during game play when other players go to the game.

ANIMATION: The animation portion of this tab allows users to animate rigs or other parts of the game during play. This allows usually non-moving parts to move when they're clicked on.

ACTION	DESCRIPTION
ANIMATION EDITOR	Go here to select a rig to animate. Remember, certain scripts running on your game could experience unwanted effects when you animate certain rigs in the game. Keep this in mind while adding animations as something you may encounter.
RIG BUILDER	Choose from a BLOCK, MESH, MAN or WOMAN to put in the game and animate. You would use this feature before using the animation editor. Then, you can click on one of these rigs to create an animation with them.

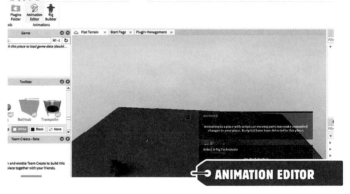

ANIMATION EDITOR

When it comes to adding rigs, as well as animating them to make the game work as you'd like it to, the scripts that are running in the background are going to make all the difference. You want to make sure that you're not clashing with one of them.

This is why it's important to go back and test the world out once you add the animations to the script. First run a diagnostics test, and then run through and test the actual game play within the editor before you go live with the game. This tab is especially useful when you want to add additional plugins that are going to enhance game play. Just remember that even without plugins it's possible your game will run just fine with the existing scripts.

Now that you know how to create a world using the tabs in the editing mode, you should figure out what you might want to create or what you would like to do in the world or game.

In the next chapter we'll help you come up with ideas for your very own game with some suggestions to get you started. The options are endless when it comes to making your own game, so be creative and enjoy the process!

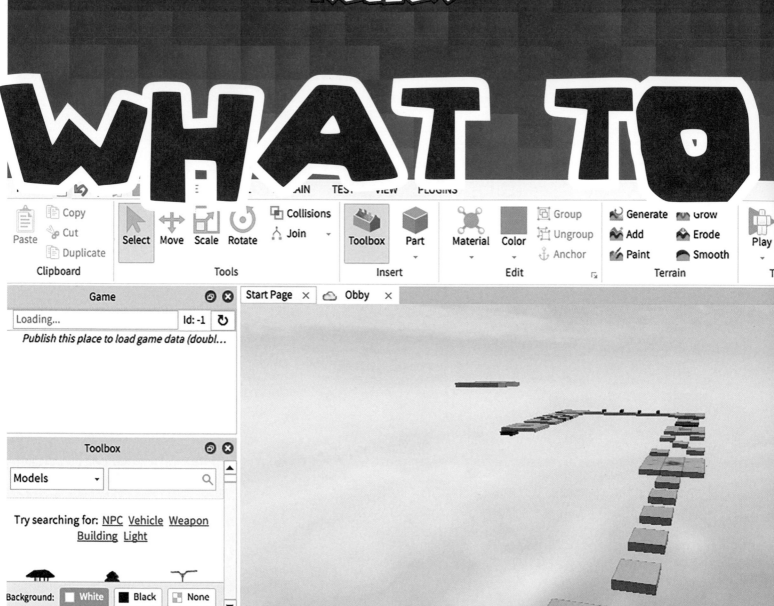

DO IN YOUR WORLD

Filter workspace (t+X)

▶ Workspace
   s

   🔲 Star
   📁 StarterPack
▶ 📁 StarterPlayer
   🔊 SoundService
   💬 Chat
   🟦 HttpService
   🟦 InsertService

Properties 📑 ✖

Filter Properties (Ctrl+Shift+P)

You want to create your own world, what should you make?

The game needs 3 or more players to start

> | Level | Username
> | 1 | RobloxFun1233

RobloxFun12333
Account <13

Badge Awarded
RobloxFun12333 wor
Hidden Developers's

WHAT TO DO IN YOUR WORLD

There are some serious benefits that come along with creating your own world. Not only can you be as creative as possible, but you choose what happens, who can come into the world and what extras you add there. By choosing specific terrain options you can start with a blank world or start with a specific area biome that you can build on, depending on what it is you want to make.

When you open the editor you'll have every option you need to create any type of world you want, no matter what crazy ideas or creations you have running through your mind — they can all become a reality!

Here are some ideas to get you started on the right creative path to crafting a new world or even a full game. You can use one of these options, or go on your own to create something that is entirely unique. It's all up to you what you do.

Have fun with it and don't worry about making something someone already made, or making something that you might think other people won't like.

This is your world, it should be made to showcase something you like!

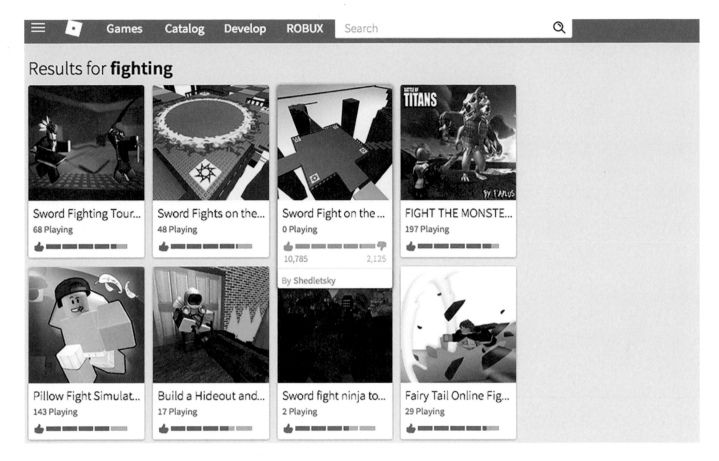

FIGHTING GAMES

One of the most loved types of games on Roblox currently are the fighting games. You can make your own using bots that you put in the game, or even create a game where players come to dual it out amongst themselves. You can add weapons, or just keep it to hand-to-hand combat. The choice is yours.

You can get as detailed in these games as you want. A good fighting game can go a long way. You'll want to set up an arena within the editor, along with the extras, such as a crowd that watches or stands or even additional objectives such as capture points or bases to protect. You can choose what is put in the game, and you can make specific spawn points to keep players organized and spread out appropriately. Make sure to add directions for game play when new players come into the world, so they'll know exactly what they're supposed to do.

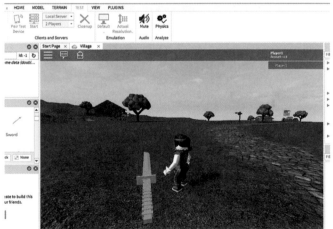

Some ideas for this include, but are not limited to:

· Jousting
· Boxing
· MMA Fighting
· Sword Fighting

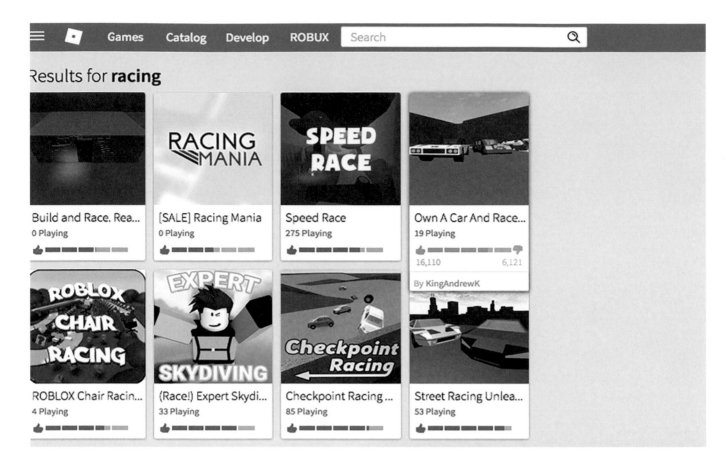

RACING GAMES

Racing games can get your adrenalin pumping as you wheel around twists and turns trying to be the first to the end of the track. Many players enjoy these types of games, especially when they have pretty cool tracks to drive around, as well as cool and unique cars that they can race with. It's completely up to you how you set it up, but having a cool racing game is sure to draw in crowds of players that want to try their luck on the speedway.

Some ideas to put in racing games include:

- A Track

- **Cool Cars:** You can custom make many of them through the editor, which allows you to control which cars are going to be on the track.

- Other ideas might include a concession stand and seating for spectators.

Racing games require a specific set of scripts to create moving cars and to give players control over them. This can all be done by downloading a specific script for the function or if you're really skilled with editing and programming, you can create your own using Lua.

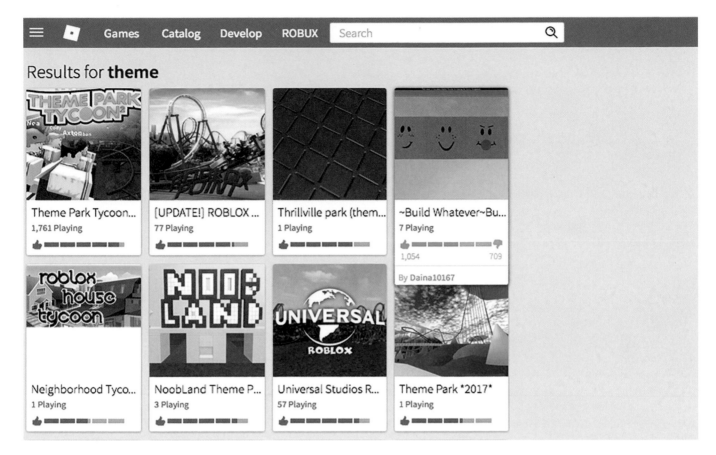

THEMED GAMES

Themed games are always fun because you can model the games after just about anything that you can think of. Whether you want a game that is Disney movie based, character based, television show based or anything else; you can make it happen. By placing bots throughout the world, these can be the specific characters that go along with the game.

Some ideas that are currently circulating throughout the Roblox worlds are Frozen, Pokemon, Volt, Moana, Cars, Toy Story and many others. You don't have to use one of these themes, but come up with your own and make something that excites you.

Some tips for making a themed game are:

- For the characters, you can download them if they're shared for your specific game or customize your own that fit the character.

- You have to create the perfect atmosphere that works with the ultimate theme of the game. If you're doing one with princesses, then you can choose the castle terrain and recreate your favorite princess's beautiful castle.

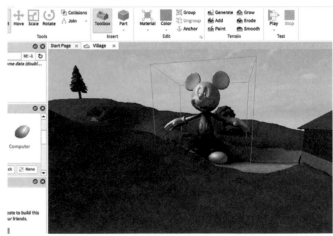

- If you're going to be doing a themed game, it might also be ideal to find scripts that have been previously made to match that theme, this will reduce the amount of time that you put into making the game work.

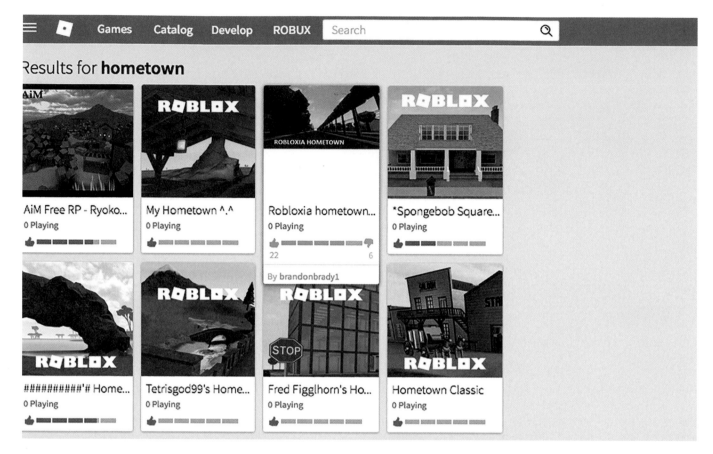

YOUR HOMETOWN

A lot of people like to model their worlds after places they've visited in real life, or their actual hometown. You just have to remember the things around you and add them as you go. This way, you have a true to life world of the things that you know. This can be pretty cool for other players that want to pretend to travel the world and see other places, making it a unique and exciting experience for all that visit the world.

If you're considering making your own place, then consider some of these ideas and tips when it comes time to make your own world in virtual reality:

- A hometown approach is one that is going to be a lot of creative thinking on your part.

- You have to think about the buildings that you need to build, the people you want to add, the different scripts that are going to make these businesses work and so on.

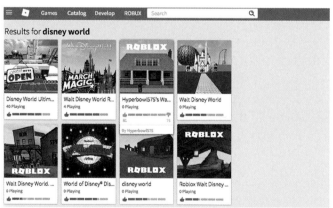

- If making a specific place, such as Disney World, it is important to add the specific rides, areas and attractions, as well as scripts for each of them. This will make your world function and do the proper animation.

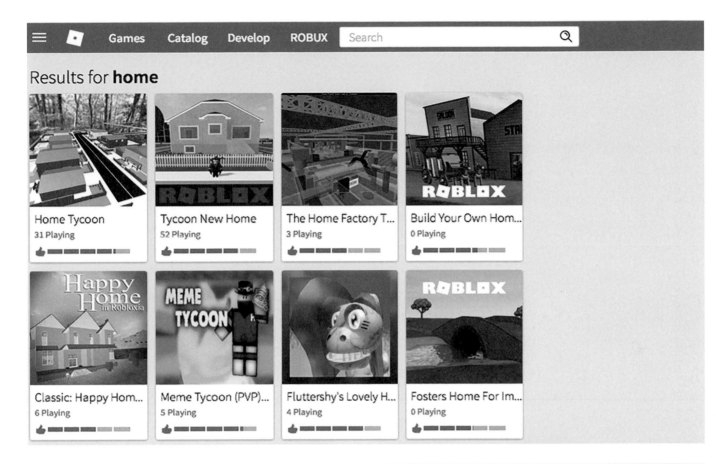

ROLE-PLAYING GAMES

Role-playing games are also another big hit throughout the Roblox community. If you want to pretend to be something or probably find a game that lets you do just that. Additionally, if there is not a game that fits your theme already, or one game that you think you could expand on, then you can make your own to offer to people out there.

They actually have games where you can be the pet, such as a fish or dog. The dogs actually poop and the fish can lay eggs to create new babies for the ocean. You can play house and have babies and a family. You can go to school and find friends, do homework and hang out with certain groups.

There are plenty of role playing games, but just in case you want to make your own, here are some tips and tricks to keep in mind while doing so:

- Make a community where you have to mingle with the other players and provide a way for them to make families and live out normal day-to-day functions.

- Stores are another great role playing game. There are a few great ones on Roblox already, but if you wanted to expand on these stores, you could do so by making your own.

- When making a role-playing game, you mostly have to build the world and make sure everything works within it. The players are the main attraction for this type of game. This might be a great way to start building worlds, since they're not too difficult.

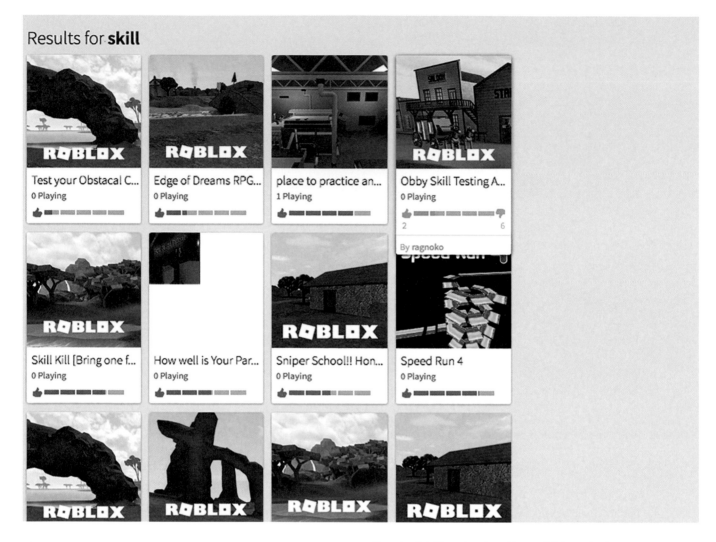

SKILL BASED ADVENTURE GAMES

These are another popular type of game that are circulating on Roblox. Of course, you do not have to use the same types of ideas from those that have already made the games, but you can make your own.

Make it a race to the finish line away from a murderer, choose to create a spy mystery thriller in action where you have to solve the puzzle, how about a nice game of capture the flag. Anything that is exciting can be made when you go with a skill based adventure.

If you're thinking about making a skill based adventure game, here are some ideas and tips that you can use while doing so:

- Skill based games can be trickier to tackle because you need to be able to have running, working scripts on the game in order for it to work.

- Make sure that there is a purpose to the game and then build off of that purpose.

- Add different challenges, game modes or levels to the game to provide a bit more of a challenge to those that play the game.

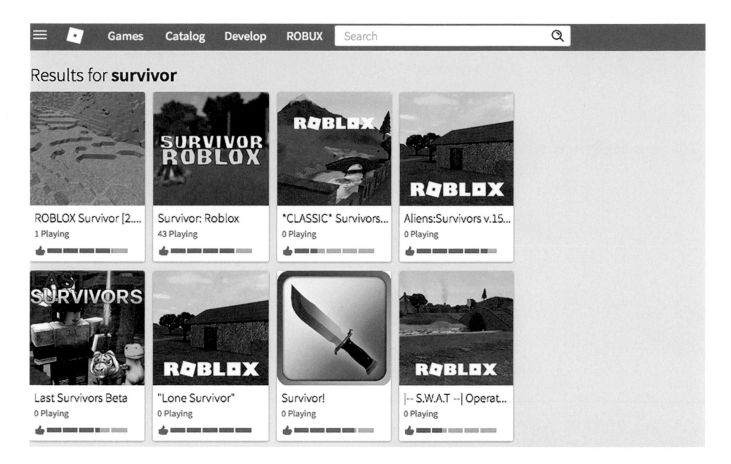

SURVIVOR GAMES

If you've ever seen Survivorman, then you know that survival can be quite exciting. Survival games are the same way and there are a bunch of people that enjoy playing them. It's up to you to create a difficult environment to survive in. Force players to search for food, figure out how to make their own fire, or find a safe base to hide in away from the hordes of zombies or monsters out in the night. There are many ways that you can make a survivor game that is actually exciting and holds the player's attention.

Of course, you'll need to think about these tips and ideas when it's finally time to put that game in motion:

- These games can take place on a deserted island, in the middle of water, in a field with cornstalks, in a forest full of trees, you can be as creative as possible with this type of game. The best part is that you can start the editor with the terrain of your choice that will give you a platform to build off of.

- You then create bots that look like zombies, or put up obstacles in the way. It is your choice on what you want to place inside the game, but using the model editor provides you with a way to createbots to look like you need them to.

- Always check out the survivor games prior to publishing them. You want to make sure they behave properly and that they are fun to play. Most importantly, letting the players die when they do something they shouldn't or when a zombie attacks them.

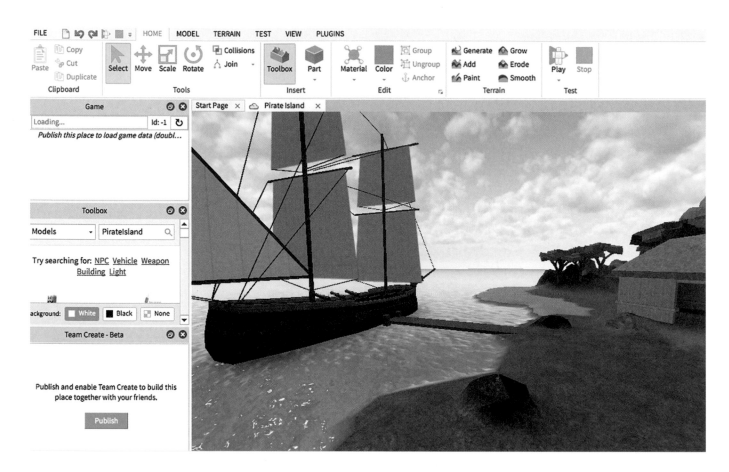

ONCE YOU'VE MADE THE GAME

Once you've gone through the editor and used the information we've provided about the building tabs to create your own game, you can publish it to the general pool of players and see how they like it.

Once published, the game will be available to find and play. Players will most likely rate it based on their opinions, while also providing feedback about many functions and parts in the game. With this, you can use the information to make the game better, if you choose to.

One of the most enjoyable parts of creating a game is actually climbing inside and playing it with other people. This will give you an idea of what people are doing inside the game, while also letting you interact within your own creation.

This is an awesome feeling of accomplishment! You did it and now you should be proud of it! Make sure to share the game with your friends!

Also, by visiting your published game, you can find out what's working and what is not. Even after doing diagnostics and running tests with the editor, it's not until the actual playthrough that you'll realize many mistakes and things you want to change. This is a great way learn firsthand about any problems without having to rely on the codes that are thrown at you through the editor.

You should have fun and make the most of the world that you put together!

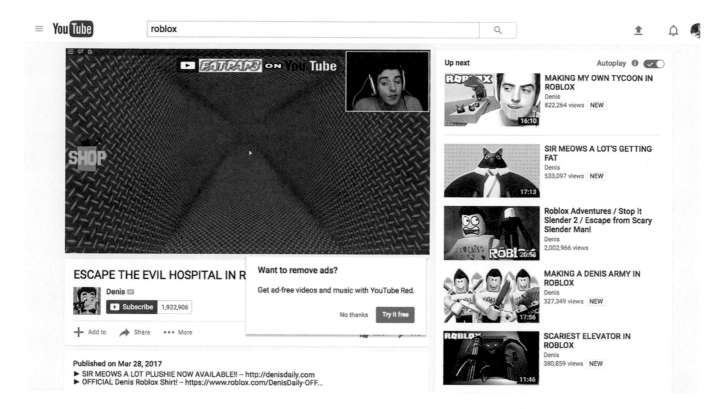

WHAT YOU DO IN YOUR WORLD

What you do in or for your world is largely dependent on what type of world you have and what you want out of the game. You'll have to think about what you want to do, and add that into your game while creating it.

You can choose to keep it small and keep it just as something that only you can play, or you can market your game for others to see and play. If you do decide to share it with others, you'll want to think about how you're going to advertise it to them and get more people to come visit.

Marketing Your Game

Once your game is finished it's time to spread the word about it. You can tell your classmates, have them tell their friends and so on. Word of mouth is a great way to get more players into the world and it's something that you can do easily immediately.

Additionally, you're going to want to think about making a YouTube channel. This is a great way to get more people to play the game and also watch your videos. When you're playing in the worlds you create on the videos, you're showing other players how much fun they could be having and probably convincing quite a few to come try out your creation.

If you have social media, like a Facebook account, you can share the links to your videos on those. This will provide everyone with a direct link to your YouTube videos, as well as to your gamer name and all the information they'd need to go in and play the games on their own.

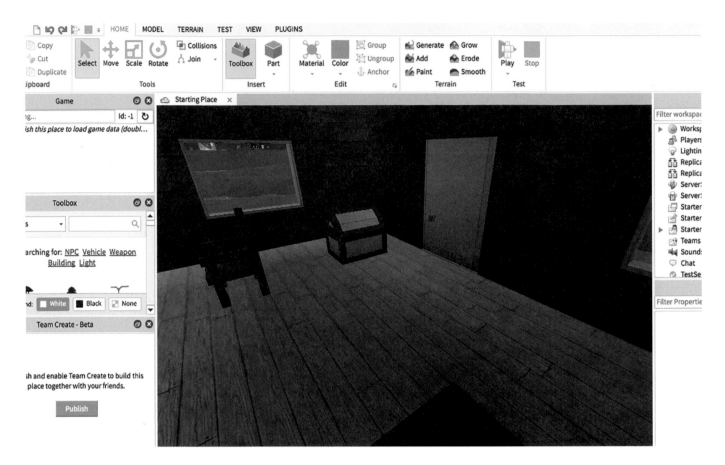

Marketing your games in this way is a lot of fun, since you're just talking about your game and putting up videos showing it off, and in the end you might be surprised by how many people come to try it out.

Marketing a game is usually worth the effort. Just make sure the bugs and fixes on the game are all fixed prior to releasing it to the public otherwise it won't catch on as much as it could. With a flawless game, you'll have a much better chance of it becoming popular and the base of players growing.

Being Active in Your Own World

Being a part of your world is something that so many other creators like to do. You can chat with the other players that come in and interact with them from time to time. You don't have to sit in your world and wait for someone to come always, but popping in every so often to see how others like it can be a great way to boost your friends list, while also scoping out some new ideas for future games.

Once you make your world live, take some time now and then to dip in and check out the action. It's fun to do and is something that creators need to do at least once after putting out a game.

Visiting your games gives you the chance to meet potential fans, and to make some friends as well.

Being active in your own world is a great thing for you and your fans. Make sure to check in often, even if you're in between other games. Take the time to speak in the chat box with the other people and ask them how they feel about the game, what they would change and what games they would like to see in the coming future. This simple research will tell you everything you need to know to make an even better game in the future.

Staying on top of your games is a must for any avid player looking to gain followers on their Roblox worlds.

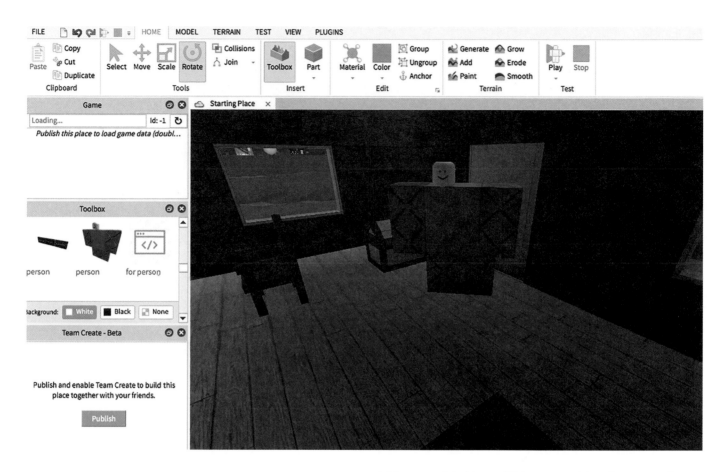

Giving Yourself a Job in Your World

You most likely have bots that do the necessary functions for the world or game that you've created, but you can also give yourself a job within the game, as well.

You don't have to be a specific type of player, unless you want to be. You can actually be someone that oversees everything. A worker, even. You want to make sure that everyone is having fun, while also fixing anything that might not be working during the time of game play.

Another great idea is through using a model that you create and is anchored to the game. Each time a player comes in, they will see the character you created of yourself. It can be you welcoming them to the game or world. You can even have the person holding a sign saying the directions. Whatever you want, this can be a way to personalize the world that you've just created.

Adding a model of yourself into your world is a fun way to show the players that you're a part of the game that you made and you care about the time that they spend within your fun custom world. Unlike some of the other options out there, this one is a more permanent solution, and it sure beats having to show up in the world all the time to make your presence known.

Of course, with this permanent solution, you're not actually the model and the creation is more like a welcoming statue in your world. That means you won't actually see and hear everything that goes on in your world.

It doesn't matter what you decide to do, just have fun with your new world and make sure you get everything you can out of it.

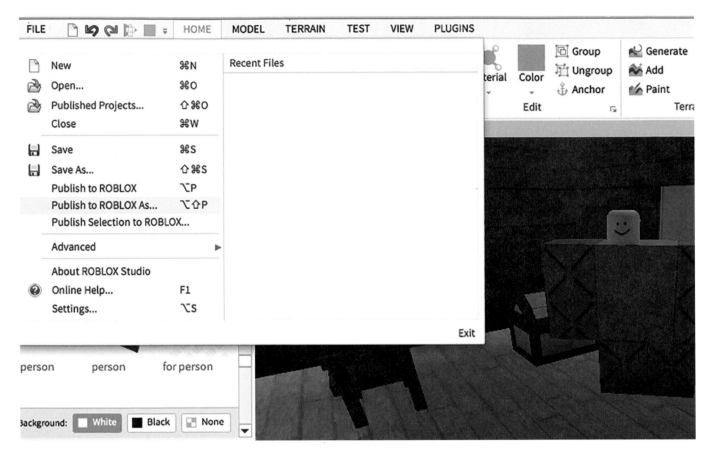

NAMING YOUR GAME

This is an important aspect that so many game creators do not think about much, but the name of your world or game does matter.

The name is how people will find your world, so it's important to make it catchy, short, and to make sure it fits for the game. Take your time picking out a name, and do your best to choose something that's going to help your world grow, and that players will be able to remember in the future when they want to tell their friends about it.

Tips for Choosing a World Name

Choosing a game name isn't something that you should rush through. Here are some simple tips to help you pick out a name that you'll be happy with, and that will draw in additional players while helping everyone remember your world.

1. Always make sure to include the type of game it is — survival, high school, store, house, mystery or anything else within the title. This doesn't have to be the only word, but putting it in there helps.

2. Make it unique. You want something that it is going to attract players to play the game. Having a unique title will draw them to the game and make them want to learn more about it.

3. If it is themed, make sure to choose a name that goes with that theme or that emphasizes something special about your world's theme.

Coming Up with a Description

The description for the world that you create is a paragraph explaining what the world or game is, how to play, what to expect. It's the main thing players will look at when deciding whether or not they want to load up your game and start playing.

When you go to make the description, try to put as much information as possible in this box. This is because people do read these and want to know more about the game, what it offers and why they should play it.

When creating your description, ask yourself the following questions:

- What do you do in the game?
- What added bonuses or features does it offer?
- Has there been an upgrade to previous bugs or glitches?
- What are the roles of the players?
- How do you play the game? Are there special instructions?

Adding Photos

It's best to add a picture of the game or world that you made to the opening page where the description and titles are. This can be done through the screen capture section on the editor. This is another big seller of a world, and having a few quality photos showing you playing the world will help draw in additional players that are interested in your concept.

If you're good with photo editing software you can even create personalized banners for your game world.

This is a unique way to show off the game that you're making and it's another way to entice users to come and try it out. The more pictures you have, the better it is for them to get an idea of how it works and whether or not they want to play the game.

Make the most out of your game and don't sell it short. Create a wonderful descripton that explains what it has to offer. Take photos that show off the cooler features, and take your time picking out what really makes your game great. These steps will make marketing your game easier, and will increase its success after you launch it to the public.

Customize your games PLAY starting page once you've created, saved and published the world or game that you made!

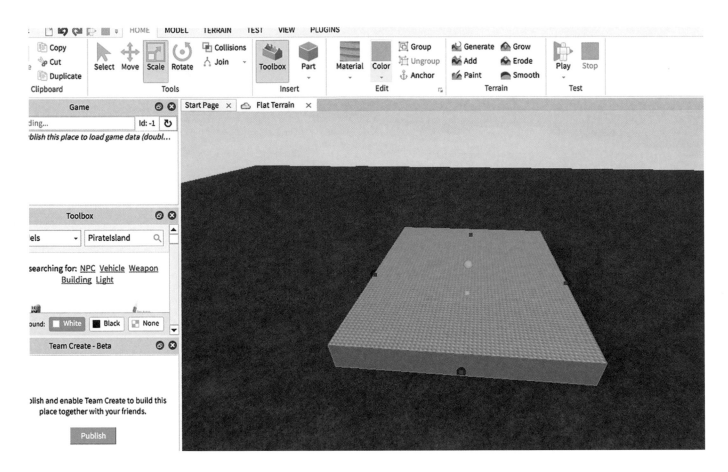

REMEMBER, PRACTICE MAKES PERFECT

When it comes to building worlds and games, remember that practice makes perfect. Working with friends on building worlds and asking them questions about problems you're having will only increase your knowledge and capabilities. As your skills improve you'll be able to create bigger and better worlds.

Scripting Roblox objects is one of the more difficult skills to learn, but it's still easy for beginners to learn and something that everyone should try at least once.

Keep in mind that you don't have to publish every world that you create either. Even those unpublished worlds will help you hone your skills and figure out how to make cooler games when you do decide to publish one.

Scripts allow you to do many amazing things to your world, and can even give you special powers in your new world once you've created it. You can make scripts of your own if you like, but there are also scripts that you can download from other players to add into your game. It's important to only use scripts when you know what you're doing and how to make use of them. Be careful to avoid putting in too many features and creating a world that doesn't work. It's much better to have a simple and functional world, than it is to have a feature-rich world that doesn't work.

Keep learning, keep practicing and make the most of the time that you spend making a game by using it as a learning opportunity and by having as much fun as you can as a Roblox game creator!

It doesn't matter what type of game you make or what world you want to have. You can create anything you like, and you can even build a world with your friends to create a fun blended world with all your ideas.

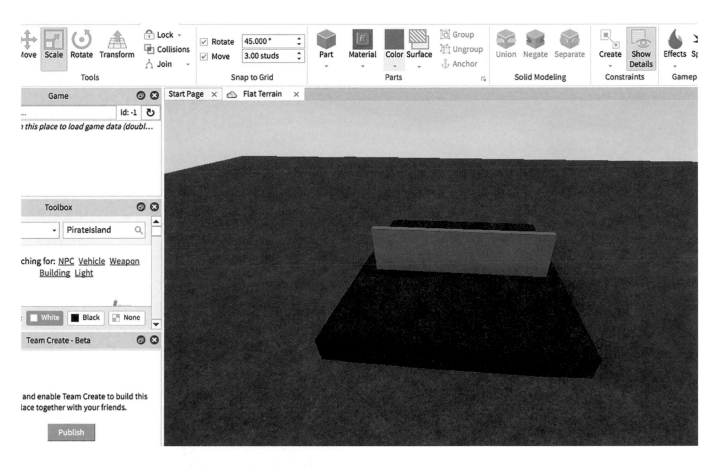

Once you get started creating brand-new worlds, you'll quickly see that practice makes a huge difference. Your initial creations won't be very impressive, but as time goes by you'll create larger and more exciting worlds. A lot of players have already made it to the top, do you think you can as well?

Start making your own games today to see how much fun it can be. For quick feedback after releasing a game it's important to check your game's ratings often. You will find out what needs to be fixed and how much people like it. This provides you with useful feedback for the future games that you're thinking of putting together.

Take your time and learn everything you can about becoming a successful Roblox world creator. Hone your skills, listen to feedback and work hard to create some of the best worlds out there for players to enjoy! You'll be a master creator of Roblox games before you know it!

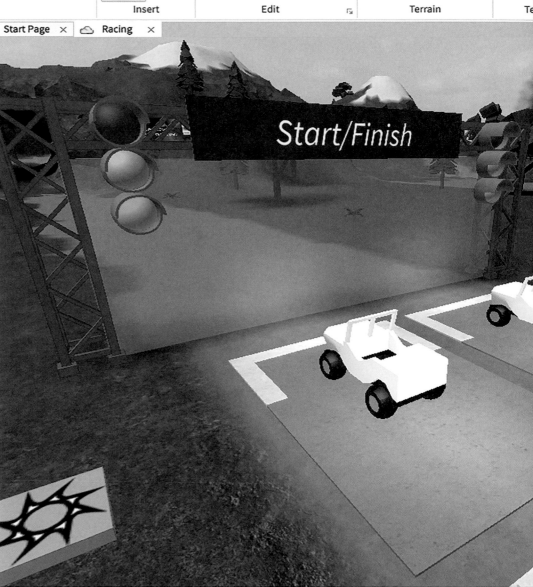

MASTER BUILDER
ROBLOX

INTRODUCING

LUA

A brief introduction and overview of Roblox's programming language.

Explore (Ctrl+Shi...)

Workspace
- Players
- DefaultToolboxSearch
- Lighting
- ReplicatedFirst
- ReplicatedStorage
- ▶ ServerScriptService
- ServerStorage
- StarterGui
- StarterPack
- ▶ StarterPlayer
- SoundService
- Chat
- HttpService
- InsertService

Properties

Filter Properties (Ctrl+Shift+P)

INTRODUCING LUA THE PROGRAMMING LANGUAGE

So you've played some of these Roblox games and wondered how the people who made them actually went about putting them together piece by piece. It's easy to play these games and be impressed with the thought and creativity that went into making them fun, but where things get difficult is when you want to learn how to start from the ground and work your way up to making a game yourself and have it be something of quality, your own work of art that people can play.

You can have a look all through the Roblox Studio program to get what each button does and figure out how to add in your own shapes and models for what you want your in-game world to look like, but at the end of the day, it's all about speaking the right language.

It's not like learning how to speak, read and write english or taking a french class to learn how to talk to people in different parts of the world, the idea of using Lua the programming language is to learn how to talk to a computer and telling it how to do what you want so your game turns out the way you imagine it.

You won't be seeing too much of how this all works in the tutorials you can find within Roblox Studio itself. If you've been following along in this book you've no doubt come across the part where the program includes little step by step instructions on how to make your own stuff within a game, models for a building, trees, cars, and more.

But what it won't include is what you can do with the programming language Lua that at the end of the day is what will be tying your game together to make it exceptional. It's one thing to make some shapes, it's another to give those shapes something to do and watch them obey your typed out commands.

Just in case you might have missed it, all you have to do at any time while you're running the Roblox Studio program is to right click up near the top of the screen where you're not going to click on any of the buttons. You'll see a drop down list of different functions you can bring up depending on what you're trying to get done. On that list there's the option "Tutorials" click the option and a window will pop up on the left of your screen that'll teach you how to do various things within the game design software.

There are more places to look than just these tutorials and we'll go into more detail later in this section as to where you can find some of these places to help learn about Lua and how to code. In terms of what you can do within the Roblox Studio program, the next best thing you can do is to press the F1 key at any time. What this does is takes you directly to the wiki page (if you're connected to the internet) for anything related to working within Roblox Studio. We'll be doing our own thing here in this section but just know that F1 is always available.

We'll begin by being honest, this book is nowhere near the size it needs to be for us to give you a full explanation on all the inner workings of Lua and every possible way to use all the different bits of it in making a game. That's just if we're talking about the book.

We're only talking about Lua in this one **section** so we've got even less room.

Don't worry though because the idea here isn't to give you a fully comprehensive break down of the programming language.

The plan is to get you started and **familiar** with some beginner concepts on typing out code and being careful of what rules to follow. That way, when it comes time for you to have a turn at writing out your own code and telling the computer to follow your instructions exactly how you want, with any luck it'll work.

At the very least you'll know what mistakes to look out for so that if it isn't working you'll be able to fix it.

First off we're going to have a look at some simple basic parts of a line of code, some commands you can give the computer to have it do things and the rules for how to type them out.

After that what we're going to do next is go over some "script" writing ourselves by giving you some examples of "scripts" that you can use inside your very own game. We'll start off with the easier ones and as we go further along the examples will get increasingly complex. Like we said we don't have an incredible amount of room so they won't get too difficult but basically we'll go from beginner level to about intermediate.

With each example we give, we'll pause for a bit and give you a run-down of what you're seeing and what different parts of the code are doing, as well as why those parts of code are doing what they're doing. If you follow along exactly with the instructions as well as having a look at the screenshots you should be able to copy exactly what you're seeing and recreate it in your own Roblox Studio.

One interesting fact to start off with before we get into the nitty gritty. There are more than a few people who have this question, Lua is not an acronym, the letters do not in fact stand for anything. It's merely the name of the particular programming language used in the making of Roblox games.

GET PRINTING

So let's start easy. There are 2 places in Roblox Studio you can actually input code, the command bar, and "scripts". In the command bar you can input code and see the result right away in the output window above. (provided you've gone to the "test" tab and opened them both) It's also got a handy feature that shows you if you've made any mistakes in your code typing.

For our first example we'll go with the simplest command, the "print" command. **Type this out in your command bar:**

print("This is only a test")

```
> print("This is only a test")
This is only a test




: print("This is only a test")|
```

That's how a "print" command works, you type the word "print" in all lowercase letters so the computer knows that's the command you're using, then you follow up by putting what you actually want to appear on the screen in parentheses (or brackets). Make sure you don't have a space between the word "print" and the brackets.

You can even do the same thing with numbers, like so:

print(2017)

```
> print(2017)
2017


: print(2017)
```

You'll notice that in this example we didn't use quotation marks, this is because you only need to use quotation marks when you have words within the brackets. In programming jargon, words and sentences within code like this are called "strings". When you're using numbers it's fine to have them just in there by themselves.

That being said you can use quotation marks for numbers if you want to, it's just not necessary. That means to use letters and numbers at the same time just make sure to use quotation marks and you'll be fine.

This command works for anything you want to write:

print("This is a loooonger test 12345")

```
> print("This is a loooonger test 12345")
This is a loooonger test 12345

: print("This is a loooonger test 12345")
```

Another magical power that the "print" command has is the ability to do math. It goes without saying that sometimes in games there is math involved and depending on the type of person you are, maybe you're not that big of a fan. That's perfectly alright because by entering equations into the command bar with the "print" command the computer will actually solve the problems and what prints out on screen will be the answers to whatever math question you gave it.

Of course we'll give you an example to look at here but it doesn't mean you can't try to do this yourself with your own thought up math questions.

We'll just keep it simple with 2 easy examples:

print(1 + 1)

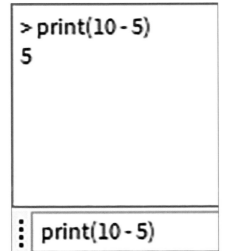

Just like a calculator you'll see that Roblox Studio will be able to handle a great deal of math problems you throw at it. We only used addition and subtraction here but don't be afraid to get fancy with some division or multiplication either.

print(10 – 5)

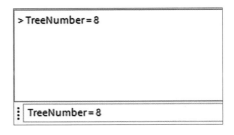

....

IMPORTANT TERM #1. VARIABLES

This will be tricky to understand so prepare yourself. Sometimes when writing "scripts" or code, you can have your computer do things that on the surface you won't even notice. They can still be important you just won't see right away that anything is different. When you write your first couple lines of code for practice using variables you will see what we're talking about.

What you're really doing when you write out some code with variables in it is telling the computer to remember a certain bit of information. Let's try making things easier with an example.

We'll use a simple bit of code that we can write based off of the picture of the current terrain we can see. **There are 8 trees altogether in the image so if we were to write a code with a variable for trees it would look like:**

TreeNumber = 8

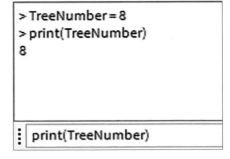

We see that after entering in this line of code nothing really happens in the output bar except it repeating the line we just typed, which always happens.

This is what we meant by stuff happening behind the scenes. The number of trees now for the computer in this instance of Roblox Studio has been set to 8, just like in the picture.

It's one thing to say that but how can we check to see if it really knows that information now? **Well, we can use the "print" command we learned not too long ago. Let's tell it to "print" out the TreeNumber and see what it says:**

print(TreeNumber)

> TreeNumber = 8
> print(TreeNumber)
8

print(TreeNumber)

And voila! The computer knows that the "TreeNumber" is 8 because we typed in a code that told it so.

Be careful with this though!

Right now it only knows that the "TreeNumber" is 8 because that's what we told it to know, it's not actually counting up the number of trees and telling us what it counted.

We can make it count if we wanted, but that's a little too complicated just yet.

For example, even though there are 8 trees we can see in the picture we could turn right around and give it a command like:

TreeNumber = 6

From then on it would think that the "TreeNumber" equals 6 even though there are clearly 8 trees. Give it a test yourself. This is the important thing about **variables.** You get to decide what equals what when you're typing one out. **So even if you wanted to do something silly like:**

FavoriteCandy = "Soap"

From then on, the computer would go on thinking that the **variable** "FavoriteCandy" is soap. Based on what you wrote out in code for it to learn.

You probably noticed, but just in case we'll point out that the same rules apply here when it comes to typing out numbers or typing out words. Words have to be in quotation marks, and numbers don't, just like in the "print" command. This will always be the case.

A couple special things to remember about giving your variables names, because of the rules of Lua in RobloxStudio the names of your variables can't ever start with a number (1234567890 etc.) and they can't have spaces or special characters like exclamation points or question marks within the name itself so "FavoriteCandy" is okay but "1Favorite Candy!" is not. To get around the no spaces problem, you can be creative by using underscores "_", hyphens "-" or just put an uppercase letter at the start of every new word.

That's about 1 half of what a variable can be. The other half you can kind of look at like a shortcut.

We've seen things in Roblox Studio before, when we have a world that is full of stuff like houses or trees or maybe just some random shapes. They all get listed in that section on the right of the screen, the "Explorer Window".

Let's look at our multi colored cube example here and see where they are in the explorer window.

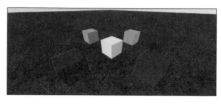

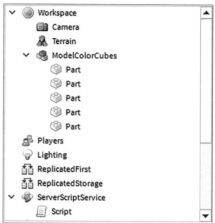

There are 5 cubes, each one a different color and they can all be found under Game, Workspace, then the group ModelColorCubes. So if we want to refer to any of these cubes in a line of code, the code will have to include every category and then subcategory they're in.

You don't see "Game" on the list in the explorer but because whenever you're in Roblox Studio you're technically working on a "game" it will be a hidden category that's always at the top.

There's not much right now but the further along you get into making your game there might be some objects like these cubes buried pretty deep.

You can see in the picture every one of these cubes is still called "Part", which doesn't make things easy if we want them to do different things. If we want the red cube to move straight up but we want the blue cube to just turn a bit in place there would be no way to tell the computer because they all have the same name.

We can fix that by clicking on each one in the list and having a look down in the properties window for each cube and changing the name to whatever you want, as long as they're all unique. For our example we just named these blocks after their colors to keep things simple. So now we have a list that looks like this.

Now that we've got them all listed under their own names let's backtrack to where we talked about variables being shortcuts. Right now if we wanted to use any of these cubes we'd need to list out the category and sub-categories in order to pinpoint the exact cube we're talking about.

Once again let's use the "print" command to demonstrate this:

*print(**Game.Workspace. ModelColorCubes.Red**)*

```
> print(Game.Workspace.ModelColorCubes.Red)
Red



print(Game.Workspace.ModelColorCubes.Red)
```

So it typed out "Red" for us, all those categories and typing just to get the computer to recognize one of our colored cubes. The newer version of Roblox Studio has an auto-complete function so you really only have to type the first couple of letters for each category, but still it can be a lot more typing than we'd like to do.

Make sure you pay attention to how you're typing out the pathway the computer has to follow to find your object. Instead of spaces to separate every new sub-category you use periods "." instead.

That's where we get into creating our own shortcuts by using variables. Remember what we get to decide with variables? We get to decide what equals what.

So for example, if we wanted to, we could decide that long line of text, (Game. Workspace.ModelColorCubes.Red) could equal something a lot smaller if

we wanted it to. Something like "Red". That sounds good right? Let's have a go at writing some code that makes that variable a reality.

What we're going for is to make all that text equal to just typing out "Red" so it will look like this:

*Red = **Game.Workspace. ModelColorCubes.Red***

As you can see once you've entered that code, nothing happens. At least nothing that you can see, but from now on whenever we want to refer to that red cube instead of having to type out that whole mess every time, the computer now knows that when you type out "Red" it really means "Game.Workspace. ModelColorCubes.Red". Just like that we've made for ourselves a shortcut.

A rule to remember for when you're making variables like this. Whether it be for a shortcut or some other reason, always type the name of the thing first. See how "Red" is on the left in that example? That's the name of it so for everything else that's where the name has to go while the "Path" that the computer has to follow to find it goes on the right, always. If their positions are changed in the line of code then you'll get an error.

Remember earlier when we were talking about math? How you can use the "print" command to do math problems in the command bar and have the computer solve them? You can combine the function of both the "print" command and the variables at the same time.

Say we are still using our tree example from earlier where we put in the command:

TreeNumber = 8

So the computer now knows that TreeNumber is 8. Well, we can combine that with the math problem solving "print" command we used earlier and still have the computer be able to do its thing.

Here's an example or two of how that works when written out in code form:

print(TreeNumber + 2)

Just like that it will still be able to solve the problem. Adding 2 to TreeNumber is now the same as adding 2 to 8. Simple math, which our computer is still able to figure out.

We're willing to bet you might have spotted a problem here though. Remember that rule we had earlier? About how if you were ever going to use words or text with letters in it when using the "print" command, they had to be in quotation marks. Kind of looks like we broke that rule there but somehow things still turned out okay doesn't it?

There's a very good reason for that. You see everything still makes sense because of the commands we entered in telling the computer to look at things differently now. Because of the command "TreeNumber = 8", when the computer is looking at "TreeNumber" it doesn't see the words anymore it just sees it as the number 8.

When we're using the "print" command, numbers don't need to be in quotation marks and because "TreeNumber" is now seen as a number it's still following the rules. Crazy right?

. . . .

CHANGING PROPERTIES

We're back to using the "pathways" again for this section. What we're going to be doing here is learning how to pinpoint out certain objects in our game world and changing certain things about them by writing out some code. The things we'll be changing about these objects are different "properties" they have. No doubt you've seen them before when you right clicked on some of the things you can find in the "explorer" window on the right side of the screen. There's a big list of stuff there and most of it you can affect and change by using code and writing "scripts".

The people behind Roblox Studio actually did something really helpful for people like us when they were fine-tuning the program. We've already used it in this book so you're probably familiar with it but what's going to help us a lot in this part is the "auto-complete" function.

We used it before to save time on typing out the pathway the computer has to take to find a specific thing in the game but now what we can use it for is to quickly enter in the specific "property" we want to change.

Of course what we need to start with is an example so let's get that out of the way first.

A really easy to understand property that you'll find gets used a lot when explaining how to do this is the "transparency" property. Basically it's the property that decides how "see-through" something is.

So let's change our yellow colored block a little bit and see if we can make it a little ghost like:

Game.Workspace. ModelColoredCubes.Yellow. Transparency = .5

Just like that, we've got a ghostly yellow block that's only half as visible as it was before. The way the "transparency" property works is that when it's 100% opaque (or not transparent) the value (or number) in the white box will be "0" and if it's 100% see-through (or transparent) the value in the white box will be 1. That makes the object only slightly transparent if you use any number between 1 and 0.

Appearance	
BrickColor	☐ New Yeller
Material	Plastic
Reflectance	0
Transparency	0.5

We could go through how to make sense of every property there is but as we've mentioned before there's really not enough room so our example will have to do for now. We might end up going over a few more later but we can't cover the entire list. (We'll include places you can look for the rest though)

Do keep in mind that just because we did this for one of our blocks we have on screen doesn't mean that's the only things that we can affect. Anything in that Explorer window to the right of your screen in Roblox Studio can be affected somehow by some cleverly written code. Don't be afraid to test this out on some of the other things on your own to see how things work. It's alright if you make a mistake and get an error message, the program does it's best to help fix them when they happen, and you're only going to get better at it the more you experiment.

Let's throw back just for a second and see if we're still able to use variables correctly even with this new information on "properties". So we used the long "pathway" to indicate we want something to change for the Yellow block but since we're able to use variables better now let's use that and see if we can't make the command to change the block transparency any shorter.

First we'll make a variable (shortcut) for the yellow block:

Yellow = Game.Workspace.ModelColoredCubes.Yellow

> Yellow = Game.Workspace.ModelColorCubes.Yellow

⋮ Yellow = Game.Workspace.ModelColorCubes.Yellow|

Now that that's done we can redo the same command we did earlier to change the yellow block back but without all the extra typing. Remember, we want it to turn back to normal so because we added ".5" to the number before to make it half transparent, now we're going to take the same amount back to make it opaque again.

Yellow.Transparency = 0

Once again we can see that the yellow block is now back to being fully visible with a line of code much shorter than the one we used to make it transparent in the first place. Aren't variables just great?

Let's try another variable. This will be one where we don't show the example for all of them. We'll do one here in the book then it'll be up to you to try the rest out yourself in your own Roblox Studio.

This example will be a little different. It'll be another property change but instead of going after the object's transparency number we're going to take a look at what the blocks are actually made of

and see if we can change it around. Specifically we'll be looking at their "material" and picking from a list what the best material might be for each block.

In our example here in the book we'll go back to working with our first block, the red one. We've already got a variable set up for it but we'll do a long version and a short version of the line of code just to make sure everybody can follow along.

So let's take a look at our example and dissect what we see after the fact:

Game.Workspace.ModelColorCubes.Red.Material = Enum.Material.Brick

or the shorter version
Red.Material = Enum.Material.Brick

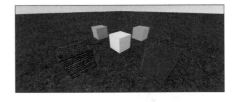

Now our appropriately colored red block has turned into a red brick block just like that!

So there's a couple things that we need to look at and remember about that specific line of code. First off you'll notice that the word "Material" is in the line twice.

This is because the first time you see it it's telling the computer to get ready because you want to change what this particular block is made out of.

The second time you see it is because even though you don't see it in the explorer window on the right, it's following the "pathway" to look within the program to see where the material "brick" is located. It works the same for when you have to do the whole run around just to tell the computer where one of your colored blocks is at. This time it's looking for a material in its own internal memory list of materials rather that look at a list of things that you can add to and change yourself.

So that'll be the challenge for you yourself to get done here, locate the other 4 colored blocks on the list if you have them up there like we do and try to find another material to turn each one into by using code in the command bar. You can make the rest made out of the same stuff or you can have a look through the list of materials yourself when it pops up in the code writing to pick a different one for each block. Just see if you can get it done without an example to follow.

Be careful when you're deciding on what material to use when you're changing the materials of certain blocks or items. In the big list of materials the game had stored away some of them are usable on the terrain only. Meaning that if you try to apply a material meant for the terrain to a block, the block will just turn invisible. So if this happens to you just use another material instead.

Here's a list of materials that can be used for blocks: Brick, Cobblestone, Concrete, CorrodedMetal, Diamond Plate, Fabric, Foil, Granite, Grass, Ice, Marble, Metal, Neon, Pebble, Plastic, Sand, Slate, SmoothPlastic, Wood WoodPlanks.

Here's a list of Materials that can't be used for blocks: Air, Water, Rock, Glacier, Snow, Sandstone, Mud, Basalt, Ground, CrackedLava, Asphalt, LeafyGrass, Salt, Limestone, Pavement.

So what we've learned so far when it comes to writing out a code, at least for the stuff we've covered, is that the first part of the code is for telling the computer what we want to affect or change, and where to find that thing we want to affect or change. Like in our last code **"game. Workspace.ModelColorCubes.Red. Material = Enum.Material.Brick"** the first part, **"game.Workspace. ModelColorCubes.Red.Material"** is what we want to affect, meaning the red block, and showing where to find it, which is under ModelColorCubes which is under Workspace, which is under Game. So it works a little funny, because even though you know what you want to change/ affect, the computer doesn't, and you have to speak its language in order to tell it. That's why you have to go through all those steps in a code to explain where things are. That is of course unless you get really smart with making some variables.

So we've done transparency and now we've done changing the material, it seems like the next best thing to see if we can change would be the color of these objects. It might be a bit challenging but after all we've gone through so far chances are it'll be relatively easier to figure out now.

That being said there is going to be something a little different about this command compared to the others. Why don't we take a look and see what that special difference is.

So let's go back to our colored cube world and this time we'll do something about the orange block at the back. Let's say we want to change it to purple for example. **Here's what the code looks like in order to make that happen:**

Game.Workspace. ModelColorCubes.Orange. BrickColor = BrickColor. New("Eggplant")

As you can see things got a little weird this time. When you were typing it out and got to the second "BrickColor" when you pressed the period key you probably saw a list of colors pop up briefly. Picking one of the colors from that list was also an option but seeing as purple wasn't on that list we had to go with this route. If you check over in the properties of any block you'll be able to click on the "BrickColor" button that you see under the "Appearance" section. This brings up a whole hexagonal rainbow of colors for you to choose from. It's much bigger than the small list you saw while typing the line of code and each color has its own name.

That big list full of hexagon colors is what we chose from for our line of code this time which is why it got typed out like you see.

You'll notice that the actual name of the color is in parentheses as well, we had something like that happening for our print command. That's because while the line of code may be telling it to change the color of something, it still needs to know what color to change it to so you put whatever color that may be in the brackets. It was the same for the print command, the computer knew you wanted to print something and have it show up on screen but in order to tell it the contents of what actually was going to show up you had to put it in parentheses right after the word "print". There will be multiple commands like this so keep your eyes peeled for them.

There's one more special option we all have when it comes to changing the color of things in Roblox Studio and it's fun because when you're done typing out the command you know that the color is going to change but you're not sure exactly what color you're going to

end up with. You will basically just be telling the computer to cycle through all the colors it has and picking one at random to give to the thing you want changed.

We'll stick with our orange block turned purple and show you what that command looks like:

Game.Workspace. ModelColorCubes.Orange. BrickColor = BrickColor.Random( )

Once again we see the color has changed but not necessarily to a color we would choose for ourselves, that's because the computer decided for us. Keep in mind that even though there's nothing we need to put in parentheses for this command we still need to include the symbols there in the line of code. We can't tell you the reason for why it works like that, it's just what the rules of Lua are.

· ·

SCRIPTS

We've only been using 1 place so far in the book for where we can type out some code in Lua format and see it actually get things done to our game world, but in reality there's actually 2 places in Roblox Studio we can use to that effect.

The first is the "Command Bar" and "Output" window where you can type some code into the game and see its effect right away. If you've been following along in the book you'll know that if you haven't opened this window yet you can click the "Output" button under the "View" tab when you have the program open.

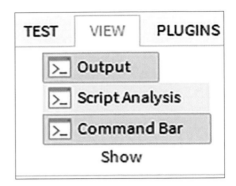

The second place you'll be writing out some code, and more than likely this will be where you put most of it when you're actually trying to create a game, will be in "scripts". At any point in time during your game creation you can go over to the "Explorer" window on the right side of the screen (Provided you have opened it by clicking the "Explorer" button under the "View" tab) and right click on any object or object group. Find on the drop down menu that pops up the word "script". This will open up a big new window that will be right in the middle of the screen where you could see your game world before. Don't worry though because the window to see into your test world is still there, the "script" page has just been added as a new tab for you go to back and forth in between.

Okay here's where things get serious. That's why this section comes along with a handy explanation first because so far we haven't actually gotten to using "scripts" we've just been typing commands into the command bar at the bottom of the screen and watching what happens in the output bar and the game screen above.

scripts into your game is basically the most important thing for you to do because without them you're just running around in a game world with a few cleverly created objects sitting on the ground and not much to actually do.

CHANGING OUR COLORED CUBES WITH SCRIPT

So, follow along with the pictures above and add a "script" to your game. In a normal situation you can add one anywhere or to any of the blocks or things you have placed in your world but for now what we're going to do is add a "script" by clicking on "ServerScriptService" in the "Explorer" window on the right. It's actually a little bit easier to add a "script" this way because the list of things to choose from that you could add to your game is a lot smaller.

If you've done it right you should be looking at a blank white screen just in the same spot where you had a window into your test world before. At the top of that white space you'll see that a small "print" command has already appeared there by default. It's cute, but we're already past that section now so you can clear that away in preparation for some code that you're going to type out yourself.

That's all well and good but in terms of actually putting these commands into your game we technically haven't done that yet. Don't worry, the commands you've learned and the rules you've learned for putting together lines of code are still important and will still be useful to you in this next section and from now on. It's just that now we're going to learn what it looks like to put commands into a game that will automatically run by themselves when the game actually starts up.

They're called "Scripts" and what a "script" is, is a collection of commands that you've typed out in Lua coded format to either run right away when the game itself starts or to actually wait for something to happen in the game to activate. You can argue that putting

Compared to before this is basically a whole new world for us because now we can add multiple commands and lines of code at once and watch as multiple things happen. So, with that in mind let's see what we can do to our colored cube example from before. We know how to type out the commands and how they appear, it's just a matter of putting down more than one.

In our example we've put them all back to how they were originally so let's see if we can't use scripts to change them now. We'll start with the yellow one because it's center stage and we'll see if we can change 3 things all at once. **Here's what it looks like:**

Game.Workspace.ModelColorCubes. Yellow.BrickColor = BrickColor. Random( )

Game.Workspace.ModelColorCubes. Yellow.Transparency = .5

Game.Workspace. ModelColorCubes.Yellow.Material = Enum.Material.Slate

Wowsers, 3 things at once is quite the step up. Yet something seems a little off doesn't it? You've typed out the code, pressed enter at the end yet nothing has happened yet. Roblox Studio isn't broken so don't panic. Now that we're actually working with "scripts" instead of the command bar we can't just expect to press enter and watch them do their

thing in the "Output" window. Like we mentioned before "scripts" are activated when the game starts or when something happens in game. That doesn't mean we actually have to turn our game all the way on but in Roblox Studio as you might already know there's the "Test" option. There's also the "Test" tab there to make things easier.

In the "Test" tab you'll see the "Play" button which will start the game with your character in it. (There's a "Play" button under the "home" tab as well.) Any of the scripts you have written out at that point will activate as soon as you

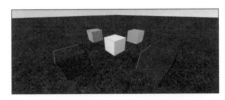

click it. So why don't we have a go at it and see if our code worked? Success! Our first script worked!

Our orange plastic, opaque block changed into one that is fawn brown, made from the "slate" material and is now half-transparent all at once when our game starts.

SCRIPTS, VARIABLES, AND OUR COLORED CUBES

However given all that we learned it's possible to do better isn't it? We've made use of some of the things we've covered so far but there's some stuff we're missing out on. What we didn't use this first time writing scripts were any variables. We don't necessarily need to but still, it's probably worth it to make sure we're not out of practice.

Let's make for ourselves some shortcuts for the colored cubes so that every time we want to tell the computer to do something to one of them we don't have to write out that whole line of code. We've done it with a couple before but because we can now have multiple lines of code activate at the same time why don't we make variables for them all?

We'll include our example here but why don't you see if you can figure out how to get this done on your own first? Just as a test on what you've learned so far.

Here's what it looks like when we did it:

local Red = Game.Workspace. ModelColorCubes.Red

local Orange = Game.Workspace. ModelColorCubes.Orange

local Yellow = Game.Workspace. ModelColorCubes.Yellow

local Green = Game.Workspace. ModelColorCubes.Green

```
local Blue = Game.Workspace.
ModelColorCubes.Blue

Yellow.BrickColor = BrickColor.
Random( )

Yellow.Transparency = .5

Yellow.Material = Enum.Material.
Slate
```

You'll probably notice that there's something added extra to the code we're using for variables this time. The word "local" that shows up in blue.

Before, we didn't have to add that because we were using the "command bar" however now that we're using "scripts", that word has to come in front for certain situations, variables being one of those situations. The reason for that is because when we're typing out code and commands in the "command bar" in our Roblox Studio, the program knows that we're speaking directly to our own computer, because it's obvious. Who else would be giving these commands on your own computer if not you?

Things are different with "scripts". What you can do with "scripts" is copy and paste them, or save them in a file to go take somewhere else so we have to add the word "local" when making variables so the computer who uses that "script" from now on knows that these variables will be applied locally to the computer that runs that specific script. It might not be the computer where the script

actually came from, it could be any computer. Those variables will be local to the computer that runs the "script" and will remain that way.

This also means that you'll only need to use the word "local" once. The first time you use that variable and that's it, any other time you're writing out code in the script that will use that variable you won't need to have the word "local" out in front again.

Say you created a game where at the start of the game everyone who was playing together gets a sword, and because it's your game you wrote a script that gave everyone their own sword. There would be some code in there somewhere that had "local" at the beginning of it to let the computer of anyone else playing know that their character should have a sword.

It shows up in blue because it's one of the special keywords in Roblox Studio. There's a list of them which we'll include, each one doing a different thing but like we mentioned before there won't be enough room to go over everything so we're only going to cover a couple. (It's not hard to look up what the rest do)

Roblox Studio Keywords
(These words show up in Blue when typed in scripts):

and, break, do, else, elseif, end, false, for, function, if, in, local, nil, not, or, repeat, return, then, true, until, while.

There we have it, all those variables we put down at once only have to be typed out the one time. Because of that, for as long as the game continues to run, it will always know of those shortcuts so whenever we want to refer to one of the colored cubes from now on with any other code, all we have to do is type out their color by itself and we're good to go.

That means if we wanted to add similar effects to the rest of the blocks, while only using the shortened version of the code, we can easily do so. So why don't we give that a try while we're at it?

```
Red.BrickColor = BrickColor.
Random( )

Red.Transparency = .5

Red.Material = Enum.Material.
DiamondPlate


Orange.BrickColor = BrickColor.
Random( )

Orange.Transparency = .5

Orange.Material = Enum.Material.Ice


Green.BrickColor = BrickColor.
Random( )

Green.Transparency = .5

Green.Material = Enum.Material.Brick


Blue.BrickColor = BrickColor.
Random( )

Blue.Transparency = .5

Blue.Material = Enum.Material.
WoodPlanks
```

There's only so many times we can do this and pretend like it's still surprising. Once again we can see the magic of scripts as we have multiple lines of code running all at the same time. Some running in the background that we don't really take notice of, and some changing things right before our very eyes as we start the game.

Because we've moved onto working with scripts a whole new world of things opens up for us in terms of what we can do with code writing, literally. You can see it when you press the "play" button it's a big digital world depending on how you decided it should look. A big part of what opens up this new figurative world is the fact that these scripts and code will run when the game starts and there's practically no limit to all the different functions we can have working together in harmony to create a game that's fun to play.

· ·

SCRIPTS WITH A FUNCTION

Let's use our newfound knowledge to explore some functions with that addition of a new command to our arsenal. This one will be a stable of open world, sandbox, and survival games.

We'll use it to mimic somewhat how things happen in the real world. No doubt you've heard about it before, in the gaming scene it's referred to as the "Day/Night Cycle".

Just like in a multitude of popular games out there we can change how the "Day/Night Cycle" occurs in our very own game world. Because this will be more of an "effect" we'll be writing code for, rather than changing the properties or something to do with a block, the code is going to look a little different. With that in mind make sure to pay attention so when you're typing things out yourself you don't get any errors.

It's a new type of code we'll be writing but in a lot of ways it's kind of familiar, and even the unfamiliar parts aren't that difficult to understand. We're also going to have to take this in steps, there's more than one thing to learn before we go all out and make a "Day/Night Cycle". That being said, the first step is learning to actually set the time within our game with code. **So here's what that looks like:**

*Game.Lighting: SetMinutesAfterMidnight(7 * 60)*

Couple things weird about this one but they're easy enough to understand. First weird thing is that there's a colon (:) all of a sudden instead of a period. That's because what we're changing is a function of the game rather than a property of a couple colored blocks. So just remember that from now on, changing a property=using a period(.), changing a function=using a colon(:).

The second thing you'll notice is what went into the parentheses at the end of the line of code. We put some numbers in there sure, we've done that before. But the new thing to see is the little star symbol (*) we get by using the keyboard shortcut "Shift+8". Again, also easy to understand if you think about it in the right way.

The command was to set the game time to a certain amount of minutes after midnight. How many minutes are in an hour? 60. In this instance the star symbol (*) means to multiply so what's actually happening when the script runs during the game is it's saying "add 7 hours" (or 7 x 60) onto midnight which is why in the 2 pictures it goes from being the afternoon with the sun overhead to early morning with the sun lower in the sky. So all you really need to change here to affect

the time of day is the 7. Change it to any number you want in this same code to see how the time of day will change with it.

The next step is to actually have the sun move through the sky as the game is running. Which means we'll have to have multiple commands in multiple lines of code written out in our script before we try another test.

Again, things are probably going to look a little different than you might imagine so we'll show you the example first and then explain why the code looks the way it does.

*Game.Lighting:SetMinutes AfterMidnight(1 * 60)*

wait(1)

*Game.Lighting:SetMinutes AfterMidnight(2 * 60)*

wait(1)

*Game.Lighting:SetMinutes AfterMidnight(3 * 60)*

wait(1)

*Game.Lighting:SetMinutes AfterMidnight(4 * 60)*

wait(1)

*Game.Lighting:SetMinutes AfterMidnight(5 * 60)*

wait(1)

*Game.Lighting:SetMinutes AfterMidnight(6 * 60)*

wait(1)

*Game.Lighting:SetMinutes AfterMidnight(7 * 60)*

wait(1)

*Game.Lighting:SetMinutes AfterMidnight(8 * 60)*

wait(1)

*Game.Lighting:SetMinutes AfterMidnight(9 * 60)*

wait(1)

*Game.Lighting:SetMinutes AfterMidnight(10 * 60)*

wait(1)

*Game.Lighting:SetMinutes AfterMidnight(11 * 60)*

wait(1)

*Game.Lighting:SetMinutes AfterMidnight(12 * 60)*

Whoof. This was our biggest one yet. Even though it was so big a lot of it is kind of the same. It still does what we want it to, that being taking it from 1 hour past midnight all the way to 12 hours past midnight so really the best way to deal with a big repeating line of code like this is by using the Copy/Paste function.

It might seem like a lot to take in but it's pretty much just the last command we used, repeated 12 times. Except for those spaces in between where you can see the "Wait" commands. There's a good reason those "wait" commands are there.

To put it simply, computers are really fast. Even if your computer isn't all that great, when it's running commands and scripts in Roblox Studio your computer can plow through those commands faster than you can even blink.

That means that if we just had those "SetMinutesAfterMidnight" commands in there by themselves the game would go through the commands so fast it would seem like it instantly went all the way to the end of the line which would be 12 hours after midnight, making it the middle of the day immediately.

The "wait" commands like you see there work a lot like the "print" command we first learned about. You tell it to wait, then put in parentheses the amount of time you want it to wait for. In this case we said we wanted it to wait for (1) after each time the time of day would change. It goes by seconds so that 1 second pause is still going to make the entire process take about 12 seconds. Of course that's a number you can change yourself, so if you wanted the day to go by in 12 minutes just change that (1) to (60).

We hope you'll forgive us for not including pictures for the whole process but it's easy enough to see yourself if you input the script into your game as you see it here. After you input the script just click the "play" button and watch the day fly by in 12 seconds.

We're going to get into the most complicated bit there has been so far. The point of the next bit of code we'll be writing will be to make sure that this cycle of day and night goes continuously for as long as the game is running. It sounds easy and relatively speaking, compared to other much more complicated scripts we can get into writing, it is. What this is called is a "loop", because when the cycle finishes, it "loops" around to the first command again and starts over.

It's going to be a bit tricky because we'll be using a little bit of everything we've done so far in addition to some brand new stuff we haven't looked at yet.

First things first, what we have to do is include this whole command in its very own variable, it'll become clear why we need to do this later, for now just go with it. Your first task is to come up with a name for the variable that works and follows all the rules that need to be followed for naming them. Just going with the name we use in this book is fine too.

TimeOfDay = 0

This variable will be the one the computer reads to keep track of what time it is at all times while the game is running. The next command will show you why we have it start at 0.

```
while true do

game.Lighting:SetMinutes
AfterMidnight(TimeofDay)

TimeOfDay = TimeOfDay + 1

wait(.1)

end
```

So, lots of new and possibly confusing things to take in with this one. To start, we at least already know what making that "TimeOfDay" variable did. After reading that code the computer will now know that the time of day is equal to zero. Simple.

The next part's tricky. What we're putting together here is called a "While True" loop. A pretty basic function you can throw together with code that tells the computer to do a function over and over again while something is true.

In this case the condition that has to be met (or the condition that has to be true) for this loop to continue is for "SetMinutesAfterMidnight" to be set to the value of "TimeOfDay". So as long as "SetMinutesAfterMidnight" equals "TimeOfDay" the loop will keep going.

After that we set "TimeOfday" to equal "TimeofDay" plus 1. Which means that every time the command loops it will add 1 onto the amount that "TimeOfDay" equals to. That means that every time it loops, time will move forward by one.

Now there's a problem here, or there would be if we didn't already address it with the code we typed out. That avoided problem is the same one we avoided earlier when we were writing the code that would just make the day go by one time. That problem is the fact that our computers can read code with lightning speed. Faster than we can blink it will run through the code and be done.

It's why we put the "wait" command in there because even though 0.1 seconds is pretty quick, without it the computer would be looping through that command over and over again so fast that your game would crash. Anyone's game would crash. That's why the golden rule for coding loops like this is to always make sure you have a "wait" in there somewhere so the computer running the script doesn't pull all the power it has to power through the loop as many times as it can before it dies.

We won't be including pictures for this one either as we'd have to include quite a bit to show this script working but if you want to test it yourself in Roblox Studio make sure to click on the "Lighting" section in the "Explorer" window on the right side so you can actually see the time passing in the "Data" box.

Data	
ClassName	Lighting
GeographicLatitude	41.733
Name	Lighting
Parent	Place1
TimeOfDay	14:00:00

DAYLIGHT SENSING FIREPLACE

This next one will be our last example we give in this book before we start to take a look at all the different references you can watch out for to learn more about coding with Roblox and Lua. Seeing as it's our last one it'll be kind of a doozy. If you've been following along up to this point and have been able to recreate the examples we've used so far (or even changed them up your own way) then you will most likely have no trouble wrapping your head around this one.

Let us first pose a hypothetical question, say in your game you wanted to have an electric fireplace that works just like the one you might have at home or may have seen at the home of a friend or neighbor. Say you wanted that fireplace to be automatic so that at night time when it got colder it would turn on by itself and during the day it would put itself out.

That very idea is what we're going with in this example. We're going to write out a script that will work together with the "Day/Night Cycle" script we wrote earlier and, depending on what time of day it is, we'll have a fireplace be able to check the time and either turn itself on or put itself out all by itself.

As usual we'll start with the actual example for you to recreate on your own computer and then we'll go into the explanation of how everything worked and why it did what it did.

```
Place2.rbxl ×   Script ×   Script ×
1      local FireLog = script.Parent
2      local Fire = FireLog.Fire
3
4   ∨ while true do
5          wait(0.1)
6   ∨      if game.Lighting:GetMinutesAfterMidnight() > 6 * 60 then
7              FireLog.Material = Enum.Material.Pebble
8              FireLog.BrickColor = BrickColor.new("Rust")
9              Fire.Enabled = false
10         end
11  ∨      if game.Lighting:GetMinutesAfterMidnight() > 18 * 60 then
12             FireLog.Material = Enum.Material.Neon
13             FireLog.BrickColor = BrickColor.new("InstitionalWhite")
14             Fire.Enabled = true
15         end
16     end
```

∨ Appearance	
BrickColor	☐ Institutional ...
Material	Neon
Reflectance	0
Transparency	0

∨ Data	
ClassName	Lighting
GeographicLatitude	41.733
Name	Lighting
Parent	Place2.rbxl

∨ Appearance	
BrickColor	⬛ Rust
Material	Pebble
Reflectance	0
Transparency	0

∨ Data	
ClassName	Lighting
GeographicLatitude	41.733
Name	Lighting
Parent	Place2.rbxl

local **FireLog** = script.**Parent**

local **Fire** = FireLog.Fire

while true do

wait(0.1)

if game.Lighting:GetMinutes AfterMidnight( ) > 6 * 60 then

FireLog.Material = Enum. Material.Pebble

FireLog.BrickColor = BrickColor. new("Rust")

Fire.Enabled = false

end

if game.Lighting:GetMinutes AfterMidnight( ) > 18 * 60 then

FireLog.Material = Enum. Material.Neon

FireLog.BrickColor = BrickColor. new("InstitutionalWhite")

Fire.Enabled = true

end

end

For our last hat trick it seems like there's a lot to unpack here. Of course we've thought that before and it's all worked out fine so have some confidence in yourself and let's move onward.

If you take a close enough look you can see there are some bits that are pretty similar to the "Day/Night Cycle" loop code. That makes sense because in this example we still have the "Day/Night cycle" code running in the background. Make sure to keep the 2 scripts separate as they don't work well together.

The Variables

Before we get into the meat of it there are two variables in place that make "Firelog" equal "script.Parent", and "Fire" equal to "FireLog.Fire". The more interesting of these 2 variables is where it says "script.parent". When something in Lua is called the "parent" of something else it means that over in the little "explorer" window on the right side of the screen that something else can be found in the drop-down list of the "parent". It's like when you group a bunch of pieces together to make something like say, a fireplace, the individual pieces will have the group "fireplace" as a parent.

The second variable is just to make "Fire" equal "FireLog.Fire" which is basically just a shortcut for a line of code that was already pretty small to begin with.

While True Do

Moving onto the main course we can see that this is another "While True Loop" like we had in the last example. The first bit inside it is a "wait" for 0.1 seconds because remember, in loops you always need to have a "wait" command.

The next part starting at "if" is pretty simple to figure out. It kind of reads out a little like a regular sentence, as much as it can for a language that talks to computers. It's basically saying that if the minutes after midnight are greater than 6 * 60 (which means 6 x 60) or 6am, then the material for "Firelog" turns into the material "Pebble" to have it look a little more realistic.

The "FireLog" "BrickColor" will change to "Rust" color, and finally the special effect on the block called "Fire" will be disabled. This is the spot where that second variable we made comes into play.

At the end of the first part we see of course the word "end" in blue signifying that's the end of that particular loop.

The next loop starts immediately after and has almost all the same effects as the first one, except now they're the opposite. The trigger it's waiting for now is 18 hours after midnight meaning it will be waiting for night time (6pm) to check for the right conditions and then do its thing.

When we say the next loop command is doing the "opposite" that really only applies to the fact that it's changing the "Fire.Enabled" variable to "true". Because it will be past 6pm and the sun will be down it makes sense for the fire to light up the area.

IMPORTANT DETAILS & MAKING YOUR OWN STUFF

The important thing to remember about all these commands and code we've been writing is the possibility to switch out some of the variables like "Fire" to almost anything you can think of. Other people might have replaced it with effects like "particle emitter" or "spotlight" or "explosion". Only set to go off for when different things happen like the player character starting walking forward or getting too close to an object.

The point is, the examples and knowledge provided in this book are a good place to start for learning Roblox and navigating the path to having a working knowledge of writing code. But the best way to learn and practice this stuff is to take the examples and code you've already successfully tried and change them to see if you can still get them to work even if they're not written out the exact same way as you've seen here.

Take the print command and see if you can get it to make a greeting message every time a new player joins the game. Try and write some code that will light up blocks on the ground as people walk over them like in some of those high concept sci-fi movies. Make your game about flying through the air and dodging missile strikes shot from other players on the ground. It's all possible.

While you may not be ready for that just yet you can still take what you've learned here and work with it. If you've been following along for the whole book chances are you're more than familiar with most of the inner workings of Roblox Studio so play around in that for a bit and see what you can create.

ALTERNATE RESOUCES

We're going to number these as it'll make things easier to understand. We may have mentioned these already in the book as we've been going along but we will bring them up again just to make sure none of the resources get missed.

1. The F1 Key. It's simple but it's one of the best things to use when it comes to learning about Roblox Studio and code writing. You need to be connected to the internet because what it does is take you directly to Roblox's very own wiki page meant for the very purpose of teaching people how to make their own games while using Lua.

2. The Roblox Wiki Page, wiki.roblox.com: Yes we're putting a link on the list to the same place #1 on the list will take you. But hear us out, maybe you're online looking to learn about code but you don't have Roblox Studio open. This is for if that ever happens.

3. Youtube! We don't have a link for this one but it's pretty self explanatory. You can look up any number of videos on youtube to help with coding and the crafting of different parts for your very own Roblox game. Some videos are even linked on the Roblox Wiki so you know they're legitimate.

Mega VIP
(FREE $25k)
10K Cash
VIP
(FREE $10k)
nf Customers
nfinite Cash
20K Cash
40K Cash

RobloxFun12311 Account <13	Cash 0	Customers 0
Fisura0511	41,025	32
njcccy26	29,275	25
wabituy	17,725	19
piggymeyer	10,500	4
RobloxFun12333	0	0

4. The Lua Website, www.lua.org:
This one we suggest only going to once you are already very familiar with Roblox Studio and have a pretty decent understanding of writing Lua code. It's pretty much only meant for people who are very advanced in dealing with writing code and programming. There will be a lot of advanced terminology and explanations for things that aren't going to make sense unless you've had a decent amount of experience with it all.

6. Tutorials. This is another one we've mentioned earlier in the book but it still deserves its place on the list. Under the "View" tab in Roblox Studio there's a button labeled "Tutorials" that resembles a small red book. It does pretty much what you think it would do. You click it and it opens up a section that teaches you how to make basic structures within a game and even how to make and upload the game itself once you have a working version of it. There isn't much in terms of coding but with these structures and tools, it is basically giving you "starter" objects that you can practice your coding on.

The last thing we won't actually include as a number on the list because it's not really an outside source. We can't possibly repeat this enough, practice, practice, practice. Take what you've learned about coding and try to imagine a different way it can be put together, then test it out. Roblox Studio will help out if it sees any errors in the code and the more mistakes you make for it to correct the more you'll learn. It's a tried and true method to

really refine your expertise with coding and Lua, as well as anything else for that matter. The source in this case is you and so long as you're willing to put in the effort you will get better at learning this new strange language that lets you talk to computers.

It's almost never easy, but the best thing about learning to do this with Roblox is that at any time you want to take a break, you can just pop back over to the site and start up a game someone else has made to see if you can get any inspiration from the creations of others. If there's a method to the madness that is more fun than that, we haven't found it yet.

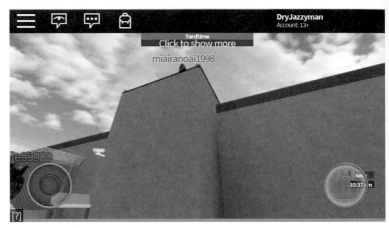

Screenshot: Roblox® ™ & © 2017 Roblox Corporation.